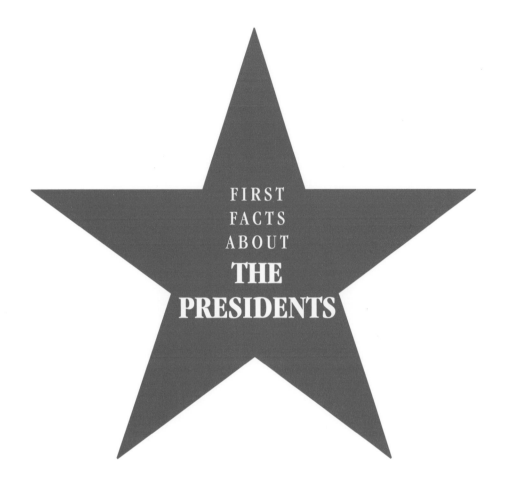

FIRST
FACTS
ABOUT
THE
PRESIDENTS

Published by Blackbirch Press, Inc.
260 Amity Road
Woodbridge, CT 06525

e-mail: staff@blackbirch.com
Web site: www.blackbirch.com

© 2002 Blackbirch Press, Inc.
Second Edition

Printed in China

10 9 8 7 6 5 4 3 2 1

Photo Credits

Cover photos (clockwise from top): George Washington, National Portrait Gallery; William Howard Taft, Library of Congress; Dwight D. Eisenhower, National Portrait Gallery; John F. Kennedy, National Portrait Gallery; Ronald Reagan, Ronald Reagan Library; Franklin D. Roosevelt, National Portrait Gallery; James K. Polk, National Portrait Gallery.

Contents photos (top to bottom): Page 4: George Washington, National Portrait Gallery; Andrew Jackson, North Wind Picture Archives; Abraham Lincoln, National Portrait Gallery. Page 5: Theodore Roosevelt, Library of Congress; Franklin D. Roosevelt, National Portrait Gallery; John F. Kennedy, National Portrait Gallery.

Pages 6, 11 (left), 22, 24, 26, 31 (bottom), 33 (bottom), 35 (left), 39 (bottom), 48 (top), 59 (bottom), 70: North Wind Picture Archives; pages 8, 11 (right), 12, 13 (bottom), 14, 16, 18, 21 (middle), 28, 30, 34, 36, 38, 40, 42, 46, 50, 52, 54, 56, 58, 60, 62, 64, 74, 75, 77, 80, 82, 86, 90, 94: National Portrait Gallery; pages 9, 10, 13 (top), 15, 17 (top), 19, 21 (top and bottom), 25, 27, 29 (top and middle), 31 (top and middle), 33 (top), 35 (right), 37 (top and middle), 39 (top), 41, 43 (top), 44, 47, 48 (bottom), 49, 51, 53, 55, 57, 59 (top), 61, 63 (top), 65 (top and middle), 66, 68, 69, 70 (left), 71 (top, right), 72, 73, 75, 77, 79, 81, 83, 85, 87 (top), 89 (top), 93 (top), 97 (bottom), 99 (top), 105 (top): Library of Congress; pages 17 (middle and bottom), 20, 29 (bottom), 32, 43 (bottom), 63 (bottom), 88: National Portrait Gallery, Smithsonian Institution/Art Resource, NY; page 37 (bottom), 71 (bottom, right): Bettmann Archives; page 65 (bottom): Bureau of Engraving and Printing; pages 84, 91, 92 (bottom), 95 (bottom), 101 (top): National Archives; page 87 (bottom): University of Kentucky Libraries, Division of Special Collections and Archives; page 89 (bottom): The Richard Nixon Library and Birthplace; page 92 (top): John Fitzgerald Kennedy Library; page 93 (bottom): Frank Muto/LBJ Library Collection; page 95 (top): Robert Knudsen/LBJ Library Collection; page 95 (middle): Yoichi R. Okamoto/LBJ Library Collection; pages 96, 97 (top and middle): Nixon Presidential Staff of the National Archives; page 98, 99 (bottom): Gerald R. Ford Library; pages 100, 101 (bottom): Jimmy Carter Library; pages 102, 103 (top and bottom): Ronald Reagan Library; pages 103 (middle), 105 (middle and bottom): Bush Presidential Materials Project; page 104: David Valdez/The White House; pages 106, 107, 108, 109: The White House

Library of Congress Cataloging-in-Publication Data

Pascoe, Elaine.
    First facts about the presidents / by Elaine Pascoe — 2nd ed.
       p.   cm. — (First facts about ...)
    Includes bibliographical references and index.
    ISBN 1-56711-167-X (alk. paper)
    1. Presidents—United States—Juvenile literature. I. Title. II. Series: First facts about ...
(Woodbridge, Conn.)
E176.1.P3925   2002
973'.099—dc20
  [B]   95-22705
                                           CIP
                                           AC

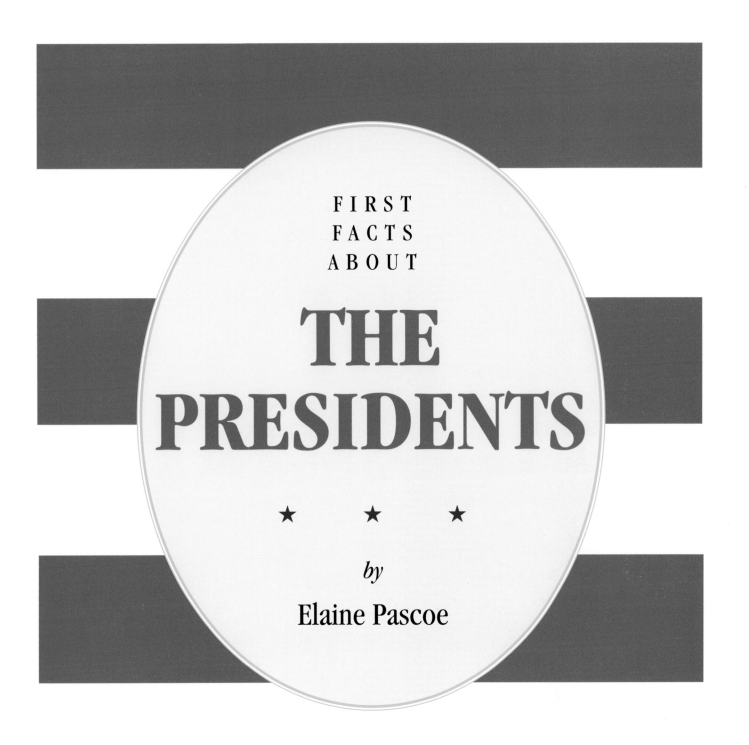

FIRST
FACTS
ABOUT

THE
PRESIDENTS

★ ★ ★

by

Elaine Pascoe

BLACKBIRCH PRESS, INC.
WOODBRIDGE, CONNECTICUT

Contents

The
First Presidents (1789–1829)

When the United States officially won independence in 1783, the new nation had no president—and it would not have one for several years. At that time, Americans did not think that a national leader, or even a strong national government, was needed. So the Articles of Confederation, which set up the Union of the 13 original states, did not call for a president.

Americans soon found that without a strong federal (national) government, the states could not work together. The existing government was so weak that it could not raise money to pay for defense or to clear debts. So in 1787, delegates from the states met at Philadelphia, Pennsylvania. At this Constitutional Convention, they wrote a new Constitution. It has been the basis of U.S. government and law ever since.

The Constitution set up three branches of government: legislative (Congress), judicial

The Constitutional Convention, held at Philadelphia, Pennsylvania, in 1787.

(the courts), and executive (headed by the president). As the "chief executive," the president's job is to make sure that the laws that are passed by Congress are carried out. The president is also the commander-in-chief of the armed forces. In fact, the president is the most powerful person in the country. But the Constitution limits the president's powers. For example, the president approves or rejects (vetoes) laws passed by Congress. Congress, though, can vote to override the president's veto. And while the president commands the army, only Congress has the authority to declare war.

The president's job is always a difficult one. The first presidents faced special challenges because the new nation was still weak. They helped it to become strong, and they helped to define the specific powers of the presidency itself.

C H R O N O L O G Y

1775 The Revolutionary War begins.

1776 Congress adopts the name "The United States of America."

1777 Congress adopts the stars and stripes flag.

1781 The Revolutionary War ends.

1787 Delegates from the 13 states meet in Philadelphia, Pennsylvania, to write a constitution.

1788 The Constitution takes effect.

1789 George Washington becomes the first president of the United States.

1791 The Bill of Rights becomes law.

1792 Washington is elected to a second term.

1796 John Adams is elected president.

1800 Washington, D.C., becomes the nation's capital.

Thomas Jefferson is elected president.

1801 Jefferson sends the U.S. Navy to fight Barbary pirates in North Africa.

1803 The Louisiana Purchase doubles the size of the United States.

1808 James Madison is elected president.

1812 The War of 1812 begins.

1814 British troops burn Washington, D.C.

Dolley Madison saves important papers and a portrait of George Washington.

1815 The War of 1812 ends.

1816 James Monroe is elected president.

1820 The Missouri Compromise is adopted as law.

1823 The Monroe Doctrine takes effect.

1824 John Quincy Adams is elected president.

GEORGE WASHINGTON

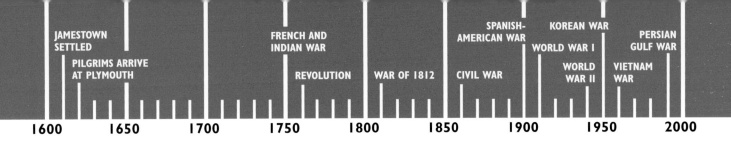

| JAMESTOWN SETTLED | | PILGRIMS ARRIVE AT PLYMOUTH | | FRENCH AND INDIAN WAR REVOLUTION | WAR OF 1812 | SPANISH-AMERICAN WAR CIVIL WAR | WORLD WAR I | KOREAN WAR WORLD WAR II | PERSIAN GULF WAR VIETNAM WAR |

1600   1650   1700   1750   1800   1850   1900   1950   2000

- **Born:** February 22, 1732, in Westmoreland County, Virginia
- **Education:** Seven or eight years of formal schooling, ending by age 15
- **Occupation:** Farmer; military commander
- **Vice-President:** John Adams
- **Married:** January 6, 1759, to Martha Dandridge Custis
- **Children:** None; Martha had two from a previous marriage
- **Died:** December 14, 1799

In 1789, George Washington was elected president unanimously—he got every electoral vote. So beloved was this leader that in 1792, he won every vote for a second term, too. After all, Washington was the

George Washington becomes the nation's first president.

general who had led the country to victory in the Revolutionary War. His soldiers would have made him king if he had let them, but he did not.

After the Revolution, Washington had gone home to Mount Vernon, his farm in Virginia. But in 1787, he was asked to head the convention that would write the U.S. Constitution—and later he was asked to lead the country. On April 30, 1789, he was sworn in as president before a cheering crowd in New York City, which was then the national capital.

George Washington knew that he was making history. "I walk on untrodden ground," he said. His actions would serve as models for those who followed him as president. The Constitution was just a plan for the new country, but it was Washington and the First Congress that made it work. They created government departments, set taxes, and began to pull the young nation out of debt.

When war broke out in Europe in 1793, Washington kept the United States neutral (not allied with either side). But he faced a serious challenge to federal authority the next year. In Pennsylvania, farmers were angry over a new government tax on whiskey. They rebelled and attacked federal officials. Washington sent troops, and the Whiskey Rebellion was crushed. His quick action showed that the federal government could, and would, enforce the national laws.

The country grew significantly during Washington's two terms in office. Five new states joined the Union, bringing the total number to 18.

In 1797, George Washington once again retired to Mount Vernon. He often made trips to view construction at the nearby site of what would become the new capital: Washington, D.C. And he remained, as one of his officers said, "First in war, first in peace, and first in the hearts of his countrymen."

GENERAL WASHINGTON

When the Revolutionary War began in 1775, George Washington was the first choice to lead what was called the Continental Army. He was an experienced soldier who had commanded troops on the frontier. And he was well liked everywhere. Washington accepted the job, but he would not accept pay, feeling undeserving of it. "I do not think myself equal to the command I am honored with," he confessed. General Washington faced huge problems. The volunteer army was small and poorly trained.

Soldiers were constantly deserting. Money and supplies were always short. But Washington's skill and determination kept the Americans one step ahead of the British. Finally, in September 1781, in Yorktown, Virginia, he cornered the main British force, which was fighting under Lord Cornwallis. Cornwallis was forced to surrender. Scattered fighting dragged on for two more years, but events at Yorktown assured that the Americans would win their independence.

General Washington at Valley Forge, Pennsylvania, during the Revolutionary War.

AT MOUNT VERNON

George Washington owned more than 40,000 acres at Mount Vernon, on the banks of the Potomac River in Virginia. On this estate, he experimented with the latest farming methods. Washington grew wheat, established fruit orchards, and raised livestock. He was especially proud of the hounds that he bred for use in fox hunting.

Mount Vernon.

THE ELECTORAL COLLEGE

Under the U.S. Constitution, voters do not choose their president directly. Instead, voters in each state choose "electors," who are pledged to certain candidates. These electors then choose the president and vice-president.

In George Washington's day, the system was a bit different. Electors did not vote separately for the president and vice-president. Instead, they voted for two candidates. The candidate with the most votes became president; the one with the second-most votes became vice-president. In 1789, all 69 electors voted for Washington. Thirty-four voted for John Adams to be vice-president.

THE FIRST LADY

Martha Dandridge Custis Washington was a widow with two young children when she married Washington. She established the role of the First Lady as a hostess for official receptions, balls, and other events.

THE VICE-PRESIDENT

John Adams served as vice-president for both of Washington's terms. A leader during the Revolution, Adams, like Washington, believed in a strong central government. He once called the vice-presidency "the most insignificant office that ever the invention of man contrived or his imagination conceived."

IN WASHINGTON'S DAY

1789: North Carolina became a state.
1790: The national capital moved from New York to Philadelphia—a three-day journey south. Rhode Island became a state. The first census showed a population of about 4 million.
1791: The Bill of Rights became law, ensuring basic rights. Vermont became a state.
1792: The U.S. Mint was founded to issue a national currency to be used throughout the Union. Kentucky became a state.
1793: Eli Whitney invented the cotton gin, an invention that increased the demand for slave labor.
1796: Tennessee became a state.

JOHN ADAMS

THE 2ND PRESIDENT (1797-1801)

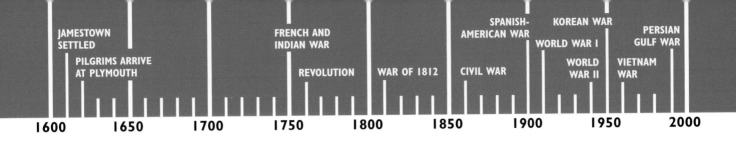

									SPANISH- AMERICAN WAR	KOREAN WAR		PERSIAN GULF WAR
JAMESTOWN SETTLED		FRENCH AND INDIAN WAR					WORLD WAR I		
PILGRIMS ARRIVE AT PLYMOUTH		REVOLUTION	WAR OF 1812	CIVIL WAR		WORLD WAR II	VIETNAM WAR

1600　　1650　　1700　　1750　　1800　　1850　　1900　　1950　　2000

- **Born:** October 30, 1735, in Braintree (now Quincy), Massachusetts
- **Education:** Graduated from Harvard College in 1755
- **Occupation:** Lawyer
- **Political Party:** Federalist
- **Vice-President:** Thomas Jefferson
- **Married:** October 25, 1764, to Abigail Smith
- **Children:** Abigail, John Quincy, Susanna, Charles, and Thomas
- **Died:** July 4, 1826

In public, John Adams could be blunt and impatient. Many people thought he was cold. But Adams's diaries and letters reveal a different person. In private, he was warm and caring and had a good sense of humor.

Adams also felt deeply about the issues of his day. He was a leader in the struggle to end colonial rule and a signer of the Declaration of Independence. And he believed that to survive the United States needed a strong federal government.

The biggest problems for Adams as president centered on events abroad. Britain and France were at war, and both countries sometimes attacked American ships. Some Americans, including vice-president Thomas Jefferson, sided with France. Others, including members of Adams's own Federalist party, sided with Britain. Adams decided that the United States should remain neutral. He thus kept the peace, but this decision made him many enemies. Politically weakened, he lost the presidential election of 1800—to Jefferson.

By an odd chance, Adams died on the same day as Thomas Jefferson, who had been both his long-time friend and rival. His last words were "Jefferson still survives."

THE FIRST LADY

Abigail Smith Adams was the daughter of a Massachusetts clergyman. She was one of the most knowledgeable women of her day, though she had little formal schooling. When Adams was at the Continental Congress in 1776, she wrote urging him to "remember the ladies" in forming the new United States.

THE VICE-PRESIDENT

Thomas Jefferson received three electoral votes short of the presidency in the election of 1796. Under the law of the time, he thus became Adams's vice-president, even though he and Adams were political opponents.

IN ADAMS'S DAY

1798: The Alien and Sedition Acts made it a crime to criticize the government. Adams wanted to use the laws to silence his opponents, but they added to his increasing unpopularity.

1800: The U.S. population topped 5 million. Washington, D.C., became the capital. The Adamses moved into the White House, but only a few rooms were ready. Abigail Adams hung the family laundry in the unfinished East Room.

THOMAS JEFFERSON

THE 3RD PRESIDENT (1801-1809)

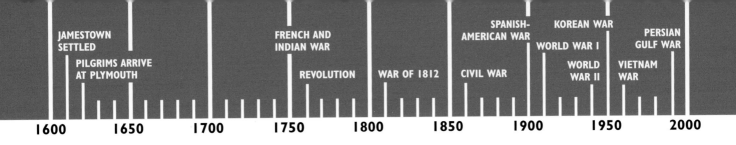

JAMESTOWN SETTLED

PILGRIMS ARRIVE AT PLYMOUTH

FRENCH AND INDIAN WAR

REVOLUTION

WAR OF 1812

CIVIL WAR

SPANISH-AMERICAN WAR

KOREAN WAR

WORLD WAR I

WORLD WAR II

PERSIAN GULF WAR

VIETNAM WAR

1600   1650   1700   1750   1800   1850   1900   1950   2000

- **Born:** April 13, 1743, in Albemarle County, Virginia
- **Education:** Graduated from William and Mary College in 1762
- **Occupation:** Lawyer
- **Political Party:** Democratic-Republican
- **Vice-Presidents:** Aaron Burr and George Clinton
- **Married:** January 1, 1772, to Martha Wayles Skelton
- **Children:** Martha and Mary; three other daughters and a son died in childhood
- **Died:** July 4, 1826

Thomas Jefferson is best known as the author of the Declaration of Independence. But he was also a farmer, an architect, a scientist, a musician, and an inventor. Before he became president, he helped write laws safeguarding freedom of religion, and he served as governor of Virginia, minister to France, secretary of state, and vice-president.

The election of 1800 produced a tie vote between Jefferson and Aaron Burr, who both belonged to the Democratic-Republican party. The House of Representatives voted to make Jefferson president.

During Jefferson's term in office, the Barbary pirates of North Africa were attacking American ships and demanding tribute money. Jefferson sent the tiny American navy to fight the pirates at Tripoli, in North Africa, and they dropped their demands. Two years later, the president made one of the greatest land deals in history: For $15 million, the United States bought the Louisiana Territory from France, doubling the size of the country overnight.

Jefferson turned down requests to run for a third term as president. He retired to Monticello, his Virginia estate. There he studied science and philosophy, tried out new farming methods, and worked on such inventions as the dumbwaiter and the swivel chair.

THE FIRST LADY

Jefferson's wife, Martha Wayles Skelton Jefferson, died in 1782. His daughters often served as hostesses for White House events during his presidency. So did Dolley Madison, the wife of James Madison (Jefferson's secretary of state).

Dolley Madison

THE VICE-PRESIDENTS

Aaron Burr of New York was Jefferson's first vice-president. Burr killed Alexander Hamilton, his great political rival, in a duel in 1804. He then went west and raised an armed force. He was tried for treason but was acquitted (cleared of the charges).

George Clinton was vice-president during Jefferson's second term. A Revolutionary War general, Clinton had served six terms as governor of New York.

IN JEFFERSON'S DAY

1803: Ohio became a state. The Supreme Court, in the case *Marbury* v. *Madison*, established its right to decide if federal laws violate the Constitution.

1805: Meriwether Lewis and William Clark, sent to explore the Northwest, reached the Pacific Ocean.

1808: A law banned the sale of slaves brought from Africa.

JAMES MADISON

THE 4TH PRESIDENT (1809-1817)

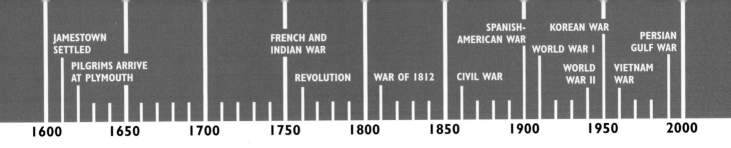

JAMESTOWN SETTLED		FRENCH AND INDIAN WAR			SPANISH-AMERICAN WAR	KOREAN WAR	PERSIAN GULF WAR
PILGRIMS ARRIVE AT PLYMOUTH		REVOLUTION	WAR OF 1812	CIVIL WAR	WORLD WAR I	WORLD WAR II	VIETNAM WAR

1600   1650   1700   1750   1800   1850   1900   1950   2000

- **Born:** March 16, 1751, at Port Conway, Virginia
- **Education:** Graduated from the College of New Jersey (now Princeton University) in 1771
- **Occupation:** Farmer
- **Political Party:** Democratic-Republican
- **Vice-Presidents:** George Clinton and Elbridge Gerry
- **Married:** September 15, 1794, to Dorothy Payne Todd
- **Children:** None
- **Died:** June 28, 1836

A writer of James Madison's day unkindly described this president as a "withered little apple." Small and frail all his life, Madison worked tirelessly for his country for more than 40 years. He helped create the office of president by playing key roles in shaping the Constitution. Madison set up the system of "checks and balances," which prevents any of the three branches of government from gaining too much power. He also drafted the constitutional amendments that form the Bill of Rights.

Relations with Britain were strained at the time that Madison became president. Britain, which was at war with France, was stopping American vessels at sea. Americans believed that the British were also stirring up trouble among Native Americans on the frontier. These tensions finally led to war. The War of 1812 lasted for two and a half years. Battles were fought from Canada to New Orleans, Louisiana. The worst moment for the Americans came in 1814, when British troops burned much of Washington, D.C., including the White House. But the Americans rallied and drove the British back. In the end, neither side gained much from the war. But it did produce a wave of patriotic feeling in the United States.

THE FIRST LADY

Dorothy ("Dolley") Payne Todd Madison was famous for her White House parties. When British troops burned the White House, she saved state papers and a famous painting of George Washington.

THE VICE-PRESIDENTS

George Clinton was James Madison's first vice-president. He had held this post under Thomas Jefferson; he is one of just two vice-presidents to have served more than one president.

Elbridge Gerry was Madison's second vice-president. His name survives in the political term *gerrymander*, which refers to an unfair way of setting up voting districts. When Gerry was governor of Massachusetts, oddly shaped districts kept Federalists out of power there.

IN MADISON'S DAY

1810: The U.S. population was more than 7 million.

1811: Work began on the National Road. It would lead from Maryland to Illinois and be a main route for settlers moving west.

1812: Louisiana became a state.

1814: Francis Scott Key wrote "The Star-Spangled Banner" while watching the British bombard Baltimore in the War of 1812.

1816: Indiana became a state.

JAMES MONROE

THE 5TH PRESIDENT (1817-1825)

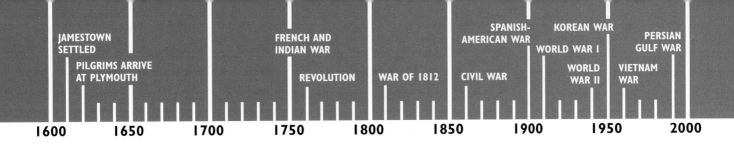

- **Born:** April 28, 1758, in Westmoreland County, Virginia
- **Education:** Graduated from the College of William and Mary
- **Occupation:** Lawyer
- **Political Party:** Democratic-Republican
- **Vice-President:** Daniel D. Tompkins
- **Married:** February 16, 1786, to Elizabeth Kortwright
- **Children:** Eliza and Maria; a son died at age two
- **Died:** July 4, 1831

James Monroe's years as president are sometimes called the Era of Good Feeling. The country was firmly established, and growing fast—five states joined the Union during Monroe's presidency. Its people had begun to think of themselves as Americans rather than as New Yorkers, Virginians, and so on. The future looked bright. Monroe, a tall man who inspired confidence, was the perfect leader for the time. A veteran of the Revolution, he was a lifelong friend of Thomas Jefferson and had served the country for more than 40 years.

Slavery was a big issue during Monroe's time. Disagreement over slavery led to the Missouri Compromise, in which Maine entered the Union as a free state and Missouri as a slave state. But the slavery dispute was not solved.

As the country grew, Americans worried that Europeans would try again to take land in the Western Hemisphere. In 1823, Monroe announced that the United States would not allow new European colonies in the Americas. This was bold talk from a country that was still young and weak. But no one challenged it. This Monroe Doctrine remained part of U.S. foreign policy for the next century.

THE FIRST LADY

Elizabeth Kortwright Monroe dressed elegantly and favored formal etiquette. She was often ill. Because she received only invited visitors and refused to call on other members of Washington society, she was considered a snob.

THE VICE-PRESIDENT

Daniel D. Tompkins was vice-president during James Monroe's two terms of office. He was a former governor of New York state. Tompkins was plagued by false rumors that he had misused state funds while serving as governor.

IN MONROE'S DAY

1817: Mississippi became a state.

1818: The rebuilt White House formally opened. The Monroes furnished it in grand style, with a budget of $50,000. Illinois became a state.

1819: Spain agreed to give Florida to the United States. Alabama became a state.

1820: Maine became a state. The U.S. population was 9.6 million.

1821: William Becknell blazed the Santa Fe Trail, a trade route to the Southwest. The nation's first public high school opened in Boston, Massachusetts. Missouri became a state.

1822: Boston streets were lit by gas streetlamps.

JOHN Q. ADAMS

THE 6TH PRESIDENT (1825-1829)

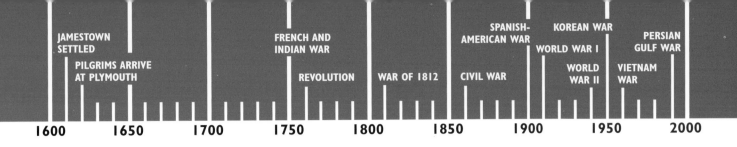

JAMESTOWN SETTLED

PILGRIMS ARRIVE AT PLYMOUTH

FRENCH AND INDIAN WAR

REVOLUTION

WAR OF 1812

CIVIL WAR

SPANISH-AMERICAN WAR

KOREAN WAR

WORLD WAR I

WORLD WAR II

VIETNAM WAR

PERSIAN GULF WAR

1600   1650   1700   1750   1800   1850   1900   1950   2000

- **Born: July 11, 1767, in Braintree (now Quincy), Massachusetts**
- **Education: Graduated from Harvard College in 1787**
- **Occupation: Lawyer; political journalist**
- **Political Party: Federalist; later, Democratic-Republican**
- **Vice-President: John C. Calhoun**
- **Married: July 26, 1797, to Louisa Johnson**
- **Children: George Washington, John, and Charles Francis; a daughter died in infancy**
- **Died: February 23, 1848**

John Quincy Adams was the only son of a president to become a president. As a boy, he went to Europe with his father, John Adams, on diplomatic missions. He later served as a diplomat himself. He was also a U.S. senator and, under President James Monroe, secretary of state. The presidency should have been the cap on Adams's career. But he had a difficult time in office. Of that time, he wrote in his diary: "I can scarcely conceive a more harassing, wearying, teasing condition of existence."

Adams was one of four presidential candidates in 1824. When none won a majority, the House of Representatives chose him—even though Andrew Jackson had won more votes.

Cool and reserved, Adams was not a popular president. He proposed a national system of roads and canals and a national university, but he could not win support for many of his plans. Two years after leaving office, he was elected to the House of Representatives. He served there the rest of his life, earning the nickname "Old Man Eloquent" for his speeches. He was at his House seat when he suffered a fatal stroke in 1848.

THE FIRST LADY

Louisa Johnson Adams, the daughter of an American diplomat, spent her early life abroad. John Quincy Adams met her in England. She was a brilliant hostess, but she did not always find the First Lady's role easy. She was often ill, and she wrote that it was "impossible for me to feel at home" in the White House.

THE VICE-PRESIDENT

John C. Calhoun, a well-known South Carolina lawyer, was secretary of war under James Monroe before becoming John Quincy Adams's vice-president. In the election of 1828, he backed Adams's opponent Andrew Jackson. He thus won a second term (under Jackson), while Adams was defeated.

IN ADAMS'S DAY

1825: The Erie Canal, connecting the Hudson River and Lake Erie, opened. It would increase trade between West and East.

Erie Canal.

1828: Noah Webster published his *American Dictionary of the English Language*. The first American passenger railroad, the Baltimore & Ohio, began service, using horse-drawn cars.

America Grows (1829–1861)

From 1829 to the start of the Civil War in 1861, Americans pushed westward in growing numbers. At first, the open spaces, good hunting, and rich farmland drew them. After gold was discovered in California in 1848, thousands of would-be prospectors headed west with dreams of instant wealth. Most were disappointed. But this great movement of people helped the United States grow.

Panning for gold in California during the great Gold Rush.

At the same time, the country was changing. The beginnings of industry brought people to cities to work in factories and other businesses. Thousands of immigrants arrived, seeking new opportunities in America.

But growth and change brought conflict as well as opportunity. Time after time, settlers moving west clashed with Native Americans, whose land they were taking. Time after time, the Native Americans were forced off their land. The United States also fought with Mexico over territory in the west. As a result of the Mexican War (1846–1848), the United States gained control of California and land that would become all or part of six other states.

There was deep conflict within the United States, too. The country's expansion fueled the debate over slavery. Should slavery be outlawed in new states and territories? Should it be abolished in all the states? Or should states be able to do as they pleased? These were some of the most hotly argued questions of the day. The men who served as president during these years led the country through difficult but exciting times.

1828 Andrew Jackson is elected president by a landslide.

1835 The Seminole War begins.

1836 Martin Van Buren wins the presidential election.

1837 The Panic of 1837 gives America its first serious economic depression.

1840 William Henry Harrison is elected president.

1841 Harrison dies in office.

John Tyler is sworn in as president.

1842 The Seminole War ends.

1844 James K. Polk is elected president.

1846 The Mexican War begins.

1848 Zachary Taylor is elected president.

The Mexican War ends.

Gold is discovered in California.

1850 Taylor dies in office.

Millard Fillmore is sworn in as president.

1852 Fillmore sends Commodore Matthew Perry to Japan to open trade.

Franklin Pierce is elected president.

1854 The Kansas-Nebraska Act is passed.

1856 James Buchanan is elected president.

1860 Abraham Lincoln is elected president.

South Carolina secedes from the United States.

ANDREW JACKSON

THE 7TH PRESIDENT (1829-1837)

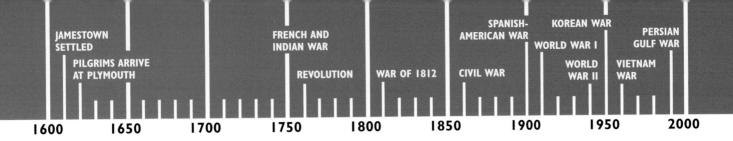

| JAMESTOWN SETTLED | | FRENCH AND INDIAN WAR | | | SPANISH-AMERICAN WAR | KOREAN WAR | PERSIAN GULF WAR |
| PILGRIMS ARRIVE AT PLYMOUTH | | REVOLUTION | WAR OF 1812 | CIVIL WAR | | WORLD WAR I WORLD WAR II | VIETNAM WAR |

| 1600 | 1650 | 1700 | 1750 | 1800 | 1850 | 1900 | 1950 | 2000 |

- **Born:** March 15, 1767, in Waxhaw Settlement, South Carolina
- **Education:** Studied law privately
- **Occupation:** Lawyer; soldier
- **Political Party:** Democratic
- **Vice-Presidents:** John C. Calhoun and Martin Van Buren
- **Married:** August 1791, to Rachel Donelson Robards
- **Children:** Andrew Jackson, Jr. (adopted)
- **Died:** June 8, 1845

Before Andrew Jackson, U.S. presidents had come from wealthy, established families in the East. But Jackson was born in a log cabin and grew up on the frontier. His parents were poor farmers. He entered the White House as a spokesperson for ordinary, everyday Americans.

Frontier childhood was rough-and-tumble in Jackson's day. At age 13, he joined the South Carolina militia to fight in the Revolutionary War. He served as a courier and an orderly, was captured by the British, and survived smallpox and a serious

Jackson as a young soldier.

wound that left him scarred. His mother and two brothers died during the war. His father had died before he was born, so Jackson was an orphan at 14. After the war, Andrew Jackson studied with a lawyer in North Carolina. He spent much of his time drinking and gambling. But he finished his studies and then headed west, to Tennessee. There he soon made a name for himself as a lawyer, was elected to Congress, and became a judge. He also married, and he grew rich buying and selling land. But it was his success as a military leader, especially during the War of 1812, that made him famous.

Jackson faced three opponents in the presidential election of 1824. He won the most electoral votes, but no candidate had a majority. So, the House of Representatives decided the election and chose John Quincy Adams. Jackson's supporters were outraged. He won the election of 1828 in a landslide victory.

Jackson believed that only the president represented the entire nation. He also thought that the people had elected him to reform government. He showed his links with the common people by opening the White House to the public on his inauguration day. The crowds poured in, damaging the furnishings and forcing the new president to escape through a window.

Jackson paid off the national debt and made many reforms, but many of his actions were controversial. He vetoed more bills than all the presidents before him. He gave government jobs to his supporters, a policy that became known as the "spoils system." Believing that the national bank had too much control over the economy, he stripped it of its powers. That eventually led to a financial panic.

But Jackson never lost the support of the common people. He easily won a second term. And he remained an important figure in American politics even after he retired to his estate, the Hermitage, near Nashville, Tennessee.

A scene from Andrew Jackson's victory at New Orleans, Louisiana, during the War of 1812.

OLD HICKORY

A tall man with steely blue eyes, Andrew Jackson looked every inch the soldier. And as a soldier, he had a reputation for toughness that earned him the nickname "Old Hickory," like the hard wood of the hickory tree.

At the start of the War of 1812, Jackson was a major general in the Tennessee state militia. The members of the Creek tribe who sided with Britain attacked American settlements, and Jackson was sent to stop them. In March 1814, with a force of 2,500 men, he defeated the Creeks in a long and brutal battle at Horseshoe Bend.

After that, Jackson was made a major general in the regular army and put in charge of the defense of New Orleans, Louisiana. He assembled a mostly volunteer force, which even included pirates. He and his troops set up barricades of cotton bales and waited. When the British finally attacked, on January 8, 1815, the Americans—though they were greatly outnumbered—cut them down. Neither side knew that the war had already ended (a treaty had been signed a month before). Americans cheered Jackson's victory all the same. Old Hickory was a national hero.

RACHEL JACKSON

When Andrew Jackson and Rachel Donelson Robards married in 1791, they believed that she was legally divorced from her first husband. They were shocked to learn later that the divorce was not issued until 1793. Thus, the Jacksons were married again in January 1794. When Jackson's opponents made a scandal of this, he reacted with fury. In 1806, Jackson dueled with and killed a man who had insulted his wife's honor.

FORCED OUT

Andrew Jackson's policies toward Native Americans were very harsh. He wanted the Cherokees, Creeks, and other groups in the East to give up their lands and move west of the Mississippi River to make room for white settlers. By the time he left office, most of them had been talked, tricked, or physically forced off their land. The Seminoles were an exception. They fled into the Florida swamps and fought a seven-year war with U.S. forces.

THE ELECTION OF 1832

Andrew Jackson easily won a second term in 1832. But the election brought important changes to American politics. For the first time, the candidates were nominated by national political conventions, rather than by state legislatures or congressional groups. And the old Democratic-Republican party split up. Jackson's opponents formed the National Republican party. His supporters formed a group that became the Democratic party.

THE FIRST LADY

Emily Donelson

Rachel Donelson Robards Jackson died a month before her husband took office. Emily Donelson, her niece, served as White House hostess during his presidency.

THE VICE-PRESIDENTS

John C. Calhoun was the second vice-president to serve under two presidents. He supported nullification—the idea that states could block federal laws. He broke with President Jackson on this and other issues and resigned the vice-presidency in 1832.

Martin Van Buren of New York was vice-president during Jackson's second term. He succeeded (followed) him as president.

IN JACKSON'S DAY

1830: Almost 13 million people lived in the United States, a fourth of them in western regions of the country.

1831: Nat Turner, a Virginia slave, led a slave revolt in which 57 whites and 100 slaves died. He was captured and hanged.

1836: Texas, in rebellion against Mexico, declared its independence. Arkansas became a state. Samuel Colt invented the revolver that would become known as the six-shooter.

MARTIN VAN BUREN

THE 8TH PRESIDENT (1837-1841)

28

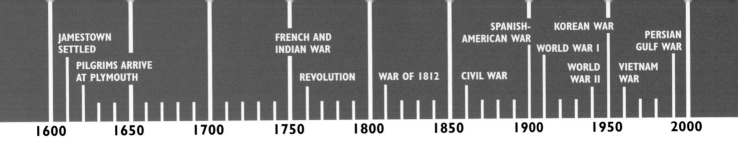

JAMESTOWN SETTLED

PILGRIMS ARRIVE AT PLYMOUTH

FRENCH AND INDIAN WAR

REVOLUTION

WAR OF 1812

SPANISH-AMERICAN WAR

CIVIL WAR

KOREAN WAR

WORLD WAR I

WORLD WAR II

PERSIAN GULF WAR

VIETNAM WAR

1600   1650   1700   1750   1800   1850   1900   1950   2000

- **Born:** December 5, 1782, in Kinderhook, New York
- **Education:** Studied law privately
- **Occupation:** Lawyer
- **Political Party:** Democratic
- **Vice-President:** Richard Mentor Johnson
- **Married:** February 21, 1807, to Hannah Hoes
- **Children:** Abraham, John, Martin, and Smith
- **Died:** July 24, 1862

Martin Van Buren was the first president to have played no role in the American Revolution. A lawyer, he had had a long career as a public official, serving as a senator, secretary of state, and vice-president. He was a strong supporter of Andrew Jackson, who in turn had backed him for the presidency.

Just two months after Van Buren became president, the United States was hit with its first serious economic depression. This Panic of 1837 was brought on by land speculation—people buying land in the hopes of reselling it at a profit. The government was selling public lands in the West to anyone, not just settlers. Everyone was buying, hoping to make money. Banks were giving buyers huge loans. But soon, the buyers could not repay the loans. Banks closed nationwide. Millions of people were ruined financially. Van Buren believed that government should not interfere with the economy, so he did nothing.

A small man, Van Buren was sometimes called the Little Magician because of his great political skill. But his lack of response to the Panic of 1837 made him extremely unpopular, and he could not overcome it. He ran for a second term in 1840, and tried again in 1848, but he lost both times.

THE FIRST LADY

Martin Van Buren's wife, Hannah Hoes Van Buren, died in 1819. Soon after Van Buren took office in 1837, Dolley Madison, the wife of former president James Madison, introduced Van Buren's son Abraham to her young cousin Angelica Singleton. The couple married in 1838, and Angelica served as hostess for functions at the Van Buren White House.

THE VICE-PRESIDENT

Richard Mentor Johnson was the only vice-president to be elected by the Senate. In those days, votes were cast separately for president and vice-president. Far less popular at the time of the election than Van Buren, Johnson failed to win a majority, and the Senate decided the vote.

IN VAN BUREN'S DAY

1837: Michigan became a state.

1838: About 20,000 Cherokees, forced from their land in Georgia, began their move to Oklahoma in a march known today as the Trail of Tears.

1840: The U.S. population reached 17 million, thanks in part to large numbers of immigrants who were arriving from all over Europe.

WILLIAM H. HARRISON

THE 9TH PRESIDENT (1841)

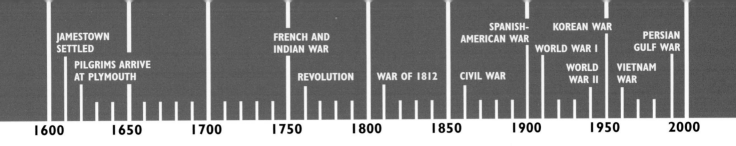
- **Born:** February 9, 1773, in Charles City County, Virginia
- **Education:** Attended Hampden-Sydney College; studied medicine
- **Occupation:** Soldier
- **Political Party:** Whig
- **Vice-President:** John Tyler
- **Married:** November 25, 1795, to Anna Symmes
- **Children:** Elizabeth, John Cleves, Lucy, William, John Scott, Benjamin, Mary, Carter, Anna, and James
- **Died:** April 4, 1841

William Henry Harrison served the shortest time of any president. He caught a cold at his inauguration. He had refused to wear a coat and delivered a two-hour speech, the longest inaugural address on record. The cold turned into pneumonia, and he died 30 days later. He was the first president to die while in office.

Harrison had first won fame fighting Native Americans in the early 1800s. As governor of Indiana Territory, he had defeated the Shawnees and their allies at Tippecanoe in 1811. As an army major general in the War of 1812, he led American troops to victory at the Battle of the Thames, which took place in southern Canada.

After the war, Harrison settled in Ohio. He served in Congress, and in 1836, he was one of three Whig party candidates for president. When he lost, he began almost at once to campaign for the 1840 election. His supporters gave him the nicknames "Tippecanoe" and "The Ohio Farmer," stressing his war record and supposedly common roots. (In fact, he had been born on a plantation in Virginia, where his father had been governor.) Harrison's campaign consisted of little more than slogans, but it was a successful one.

THE FIRST LADY

Anna Symmes Harrison was disappointed when her husband decided to run for president. She had hoped that he would give up politics and become the Ohio farmer that his supporters said he was. She missed the inauguration and never lived in the White House. The Harrisons' daughter-in-law Jane Irwin Harrison served as White House hostess during his brief term.

THE VICE-PRESIDENT

John Tyler started his career at age 19 as a circuit lawyer, making rounds on horseback. He served as a congressman, governor, and senator of Virginia. He was chosen as the Whig party candidate for vice-president in 1840.

IN HARRISON'S DAY

1841: The first wagon train to reach California by way of the Oregon Trail arrived in Sacramento in November. Seventy people traveled across the Rocky Mountains with the wagons, which had left Independence, Missouri, the spring before.

HARRISON AND TYLER.

OLD KNOX WILL CHERISH IN MANHOOD THE DEFENDER OF HER INFANCY.

HARRISON AND TYLER CAMPAIGN BADGE. (IN POSSESSION OF BENJAMIN HARRISON.)

A campaign artifact.

JOHN TYLER

THE 10TH PRESIDENT (1841-1845)

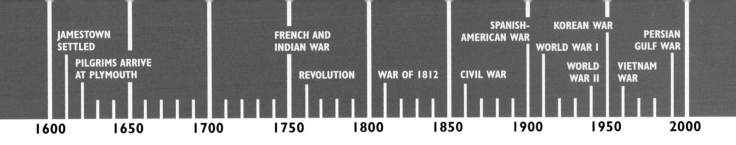

	JAMESTOWN SETTLED			FRENCH AND INDIAN WAR		SPANISH-AMERICAN WAR	KOREAN WAR
	PILGRIMS ARRIVE AT PLYMOUTH			REVOLUTION	WAR OF 1812	WORLD WAR I	PERSIAN GULF WAR
					CIVIL WAR	WORLD WAR II	VIETNAM WAR

1600   1650   1700   1750   1800   1850   1900   1950   2000

- **Born:** March 29, 1790, in Charles City County, Virginia
- **Education:** Graduated from the College of William and Mary in 1807
- **Occupation:** Lawyer
- **Political Party:** Whig
- **Vice-President:** None
- **Married:** March 29, 1813, to Letitia Christian; June 26, 1844, to Julia Gardiner
- **Children:** Eight by his first marriage; seven by the second
- **Died:** January 18, 1862

John Tyler had been elected William Henry Harrison's vice-president. Two days after Harrison died in office, Tyler was sworn in as president. He served Harrison's remaining term without a vice-president.

A Virginian, Tyler favored the South in the growing debate over slavery. The Whig party had picked him as its vice-presidential candidate mainly to draw southern votes. No one had expected him to be president, and many Whigs were unhappy with this turn of events. Some said he should resign, so that a new election could be held. Behind his back, they referred to him as "His Accidency."

Tyler took control of the presidency all the same. When Congress passed bills that he did not like, he vetoed them—even when Whigs wrote the bills. This so infuriated the Whigs that they disowned him. Tyler succeeded in ending the Seminole War and settling a dispute with Britain over the Maine boundary. He also approved a treaty that would allow Texas to become a state. Northerners opposed this because Texas allowed slavery.

Tyler did not seek a second term. He stayed out of politics until 1861, when the Civil War began. Then he was elected to the Confederate Legislature, but he died before taking his seat.

THE FIRST LADIES

Letitia Christian Tyler, John Tyler's first wife, suffered a stroke two years before he became president. She remained ill and died in 1842. Tyler's daughter-in-law Priscilla Cooper Tyler and his daughter Letitia Tyler Semple acted as hostesses for White House events until he remarried in June 1844. Tyler was the first president to marry while in office.

Julia Gardiner Tyler, Tyler's second wife, was the daughter of a former New York state senator. She was 30 years younger than the president. Her few months as First Lady were marked by lively parties and entertainments.

IN TYLER'S DAY

Hanging the telegraph wire.

1844: Samuel Morse sent a message from Washington, D.C., to Baltimore, Maryland, on his newly invented telegraph. China signed a treaty opening its ports to trade with the United States.

1845: Florida became a state.

JAMES K. POLK

THE 11TH PRESIDENT (1845-1849)

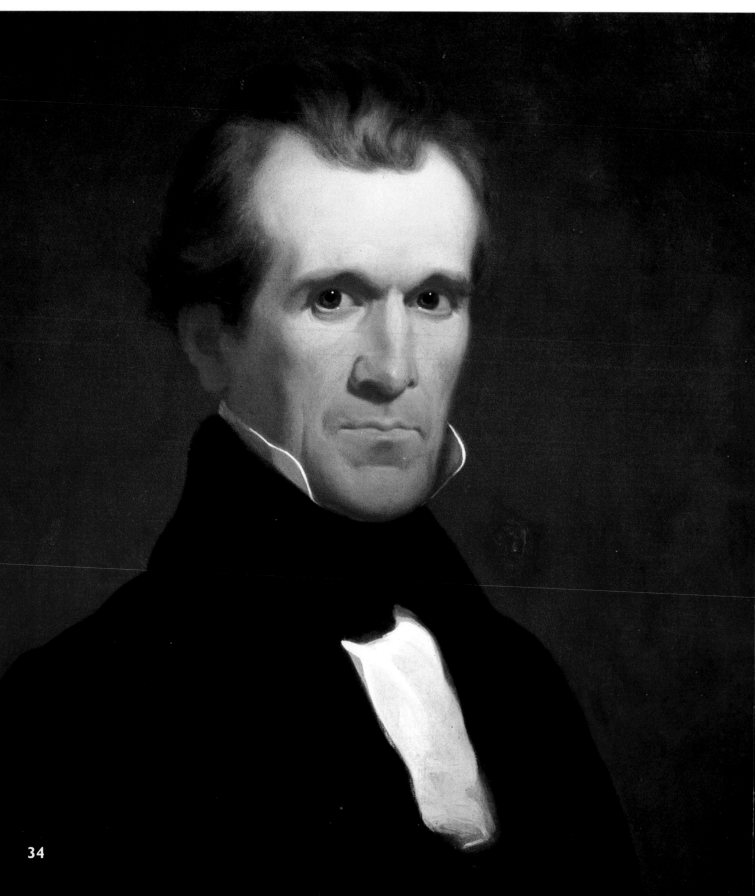

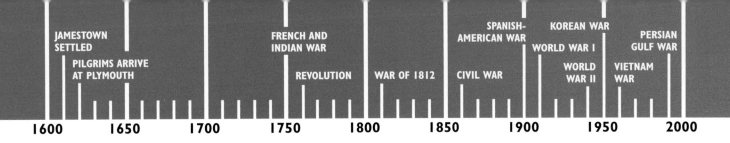

| JAMESTOWN SETTLED | | FRENCH AND INDIAN WAR | | | | SPANISH-AMERICAN WAR | KOREAN WAR | PERSIAN GULF WAR |
| PILGRIMS ARRIVE AT PLYMOUTH | | REVOLUTION | WAR OF 1812 | CIVIL WAR | | WORLD WAR I | WORLD WAR II | VIETNAM WAR |

| 1600 | 1650 | 1700 | 1750 | 1800 | 1850 | 1900 | 1950 | 2000 |

- **Born:** November 2, 1795, near Pineville, North Carolina
- **Education:** Graduated from the University of North Carolina in 1818
- **Occupation:** Lawyer
- **Political Party:** Democratic
- **Vice-President:** George Mifflin Dallas
- **Married:** January 1, 1824, to Sarah Childress
- **Children:** None
- **Died:** June 15, 1849

Few people had heard of James Knox Polk when he ran for president in 1844. A Democrat who had served quietly for years as a congressman from Tennessee, he was a longtime friend of Andrew Jackson. On Jackson's advice, Polk took popular positions in the campaign: He favored the annexation of Texas and the occupation of the Oregon Country, which was claimed by both Britain and the United States. Many Americans liked the idea of expansion, and Polk won by a narrow margin.

Polk made good on his campaign promises. He settled the Oregon dispute, setting the U.S.-Canadian boundary at the 49th parallel (a degree of latitude). And Texas joined the Union late in 1845, leading to war with Mexico in 1846. American forces marched into Mexican territory and advanced all the way to Mexico City. By a treaty signed in 1848, the United States gained 500,000 square miles of territory, including

The Battle of Vera Cruz, in the Mexican War.

California. But Polk was unable to solve the most serious issue of the day: the debate over slavery.

During his campaign, Polk promised to serve only one term. He kept that promise, too. But he left office exhausted and died just a few months later.

THE FIRST LADY

Sarah Childress Polk, the daughter of a Tennessee planter, was well educated. She took an interest in politics and served as President Polk's official secretary. Admired as First Lady, she was also known for her seriousness. She would not permit dancing, card-playing, or alcoholic beverages in the White House.

THE VICE-PRESIDENT

George Mifflin Dallas, who was a Pennsylvania lawyer, had been a senator and U.S. minister to Russia before becoming James Polk's vice-president. He was such a strong supporter of Texas statehood that Texans named a county and a city after him.

IN POLK'S DAY

1845: Texas became a state.

1846: Elias Howe patented the sewing machine. Iowa became a state.

1847: Mormons settled at Great Salt Lake, in present-day Utah.

1848: Gold was discovered at Sutter's Mill in California. Women met at Seneca Falls, New York, to demand equal rights, including the right to vote. Wisconsin became a state.

ZACHARY TAYLOR

THE 12TH PRESIDENT (1849-1850)

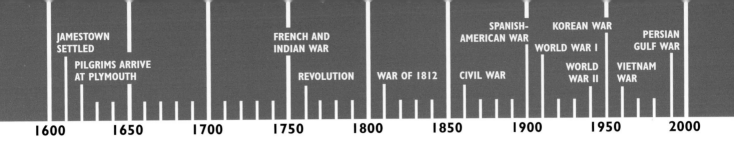

			SPANISH-AMERICAN WAR	KOREAN WAR	
JAMESTOWN SETTLED	FRENCH AND INDIAN WAR		WORLD WAR I	PERSIAN GULF WAR
PILGRIMS ARRIVE AT PLYMOUTH	REVOLUTION	WAR OF 1812	CIVIL WAR	WORLD WAR II	VIETNAM WAR

1600   1650   1700   1750   1800   1850   1900   1950   2000

- **Born:** November 24, 1784, in Orange County, Virginia
- **Education:** Little formal schooling
- **Occupation:** Soldier
- **Political Party:** Whig
- **Vice-President:** Millard Fillmore
- **Married:** June 21, 1810, to Margaret Mackall Smith
- **Children:** Ann, Sarah, Mary Elizabeth, and Richard; two daughters died in infancy
- **Died:** July 9, 1850

In 1847, during the Mexican War, General Zachary Taylor's American army forces pushed deep into northern Mexico. At Buena Vista, Taylor ran smack into a Mexican army that outnumbered his soldiers by four to one. But after a two-day battle, Taylor forced the Mexicans to retreat. The battle made him famous—and that helped him become president despite his lack of political experience.

Taylor grew up on the Kentucky frontier. His soldiers nicknamed him "Old Rough and Ready," for his informal dress and ways. As president, he liked to gallop his cavalry horse, Old Whitey, around the White House grounds. Taylor had no political experience; in fact, he had never even voted. But he impressed people with his honesty.

The big issue of Taylor's day was whether to allow slavery in the territory gained from Mexico. Taylor had owned slaves. But when Southern states threatened to secede (separate from the country) over this issue, he made it clear that he would fight to preserve the Union.

Taylor served only a year and a half as president. On July 4, 1850, he took part in ceremonies at the then-unfinished Washington Monument. That night, he developed a stomach ailment. He died five days later.

THE FIRST LADY

Margaret Mackall Smith Taylor, the daughter of a Maryland planter, was often ill during her brief time as First Lady. The Taylors' youngest daughter, Mary Elizabeth, frequently acted as hostess for functions at the White House.

THE VICE-PRESIDENT

Millard Fillmore, Zachary Taylor's vice-president and his successor (follower) as president, was an experienced politician from New York. He had served in the House of Representatives for 11 years and was a leader of the Whig party.

IN TAYLOR'S DAY

1849:   Thousands of gold-seekers—Forty-niners—headed for California. Elizabeth Blackwell, trained at Geneva Medical School in Geneva, New York, became the first woman physician in the United States.

1850:   The U.S. population reached 23 million. Irish immigrants, fleeing famine in their homeland, contributed significantly to the Union's population growth.

The Washington Monument, under construction.

37

MILLARD FILLMORE

THE 13TH PRESIDENT (1850-1853)

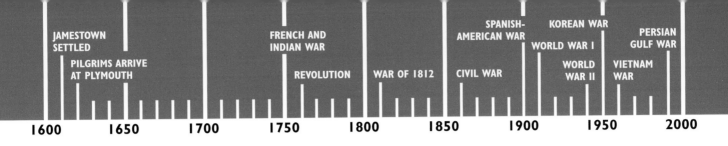

JAMESTOWN SETTLED			FRENCH AND INDIAN WAR			SPANISH-AMERICAN WAR	KOREAN WAR	PERSIAN GULF WAR
PILGRIMS ARRIVE AT PLYMOUTH			REVOLUTION	WAR OF 1812	CIVIL WAR	WORLD WAR I	WORLD WAR II	VIETNAM WAR

1600   1650   1700   1750   1800   1850   1900   1950   2000

- **Born:** January 7, 1800, in Locke, New York
- **Education:** Studied law privately
- **Occupation:** Lawyer
- **Political Party:** Whig
- **Vice-President:** None
- **Married:** February 5, 1826, to Abigail Powers
- **Children:** Millard Powers and Mary Abigail
- **Died:** March 8, 1874

Millard Fillmore rose to the presidency from poverty. He was born in a cabin in western New York. His family was so poor that he could attend school only briefly. Instead, he was apprenticed to a clothmaker. Fillmore hated the work and managed to buy his way out of the apprenticeship. He became a clerk in a law office, studied to become a lawyer, and entered the world of politics.

Fillmore became president when Zachary Taylor died in office. (Fillmore thus had no vice-president.) One of his first acts was to support a plan that became known as the Compromise of 1850, which Taylor had opposed. This bill allowed California to join the Union as a free state, but it put off the decision on slavery in the new U.S. territories of Utah and New Mexico. It also strengthened the fugitive-slave laws. In addition, the Compromise of 1850 delayed the Civil War over the slavery issue for another decade.

In 1852, Fillmore sent Commodore Matthew Perry to Japan, on a mission that would open trade with that nation. But Fillmore was not a strong leader, and his compromise on slavery cost him support in the North. He was not nominated by his party to run for a second term in 1852. He did win the nomination in 1856, but he lost that election.

THE FIRST LADY

Abigail Powers Fillmore, a schoolteacher, met her husband when he was a student in her class. He was 19, and she was 21. Abigail had a lifelong love of reading. As First Lady, she obtained funds from Congress and selected books for a White House library. She also installed the first cooking stove in the White House. Abigail Fillmore was often ill, however, and her daughter Mary Abigail took her place at many social events. The First Lady died just weeks after her husband left the presidency.

IN FILLMORE'S DAY

1850: California became a state.

1851: Setting a record, the clipper ship *Flying Cloud* sailed from New York around Cape Horn to California in just over 89 days.

1852: Harriet Beecher Stowe's novel *Uncle Tom's Cabin* was published. It helped rally public opinion against slavery.

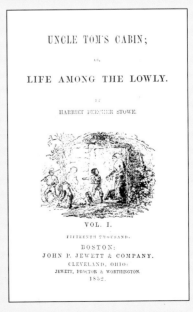

39

FRANKLIN PIERCE

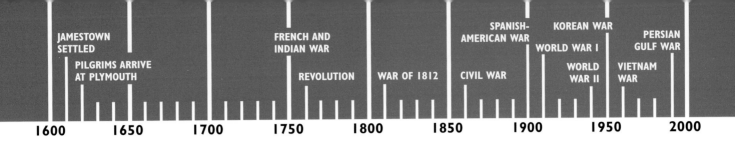
- **Born:** November 23, 1804, in Hillsborough, New Hampshire
- **Education:** Graduated from Bowdoin College in 1824
- **Occupation:** Lawyer
- **Political Party:** Democratic
- **Vice-President:** William R. D. King
- **Married:** November 19, 1834, to Jane Means Appleton
- **Children:** Benjamin; two other sons died in early childhood
- **Died:** October 8, 1869

Franklin Pierce's political career got off to a fast start. Son of a Revolutionary War hero, he became a U.S. senator when he was only 32. But in 1842, he resigned and returned to New Hampshire, partly because his wife disliked Washington, D.C. Pierce practiced law, fought in the Mexican War—and managed to stay out of politics for ten years.

Then, in 1852, the Democrats could not agree on a presidential candidate. Pierce's name was put forward as a compromise, and he won both the nomination and the election. But the victory was marred by a personal tragedy. Several weeks before his inauguration, the Pierces were involved in a train wreck. Benjamin, their only living son, was killed. Their grief made the White House a somber place during Pierce's term.

While Pierce was president, fighting erupted over slavery in Kansas and Nebraska. In 1854, Pierce supported, and Congress approved, the Kansas-Nebraska Act. It let settlers in those territories decide for themselves whether to allow slavery. The result was violence. In Kansas, two governments—one for slavery, one against—battled for control. Pierce sent troops, but the fighting continued. He lost public support and did not run for a second term.

THE FIRST LADY

Jane Means Appleton Pierce was a firm believer in temperance—she opposed alcoholic drinks of any kind. She did not like politics and was deeply unhappy when her husband ran for president. When their 11-year-old son Benjamin died, she was so grief-stricken that she did not appear in public for two years. Jane's distant cousin Abigail Kent Means stayed in the White House as her companion and acted as hostess for public events during Pierce's time in office

THE VICE-PRESIDENT

William R. D. King, a senator from Alabama, was elected as Franklin Pierce's vice-president. But he never had a chance to serve. On Inauguration Day, King was in Cuba, too ill to travel to Washington. He was sworn in by a U.S. official in Havana, but he died six weeks later.

IN PIERCE'S DAY

1853: In the Gadsden Purchase, Mexico sold the United States 30,000 square miles of territory in what are present-day Arizona and New Mexico.

1854: The Democratic party split, the Whig party died, and the Republican party was formed because of the slavery issue. About 400,000 immigrants arrived in New York City.

41

JAMES BUCHANAN

THE 15TH PRESIDENT (1857-1861)

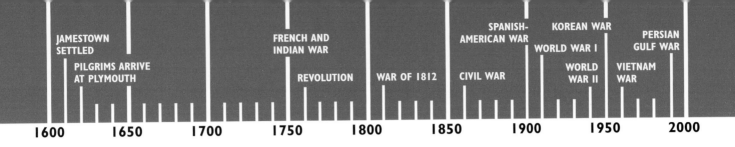

JAMESTOWN SETTLED

PILGRIMS ARRIVE AT PLYMOUTH

FRENCH AND INDIAN WAR

REVOLUTION

WAR OF 1812

CIVIL WAR

SPANISH-AMERICAN WAR

WORLD WAR I

KOREAN WAR

WORLD WAR II

VIETNAM WAR

PERSIAN GULF WAR

1600   1650   1700   1750   1800   1850   1900   1950   2000

- **Born:** April 23, 1791, near Mercersburg, Pennsylvania
- **Education:** Graduated from Dickinson College in 1809
- **Occupation:** Lawyer
- **Political Party:** Democratic
- **Vice-President:** John C. Breckenridge
- **Never married**
- **Died:** June 1, 1868

When James Buchanan became president, the country was speeding toward civil war over the issue of slavery. Buchanan opposed slavery, but he tried to take the middle ground—between Northerners who wanted to abolish it and Southerners who believed it was their right to keep slaves. In the end, President Buchanan pleased no one. But he did manage to keep the Union together until the final weeks of his term.

Buchanan had had a long career in government. He had served in Congress, as secretary of state under James K. Polk, and as minister to Britain. As president, he won a cooling-off period in the fighting that was raging over the slavery issue in Kansas. Kansas entered the Union—as a free state—in 1861.

The Union, however, was breaking up. The Democrats had been defeated by Abraham Lincoln, an anti-slavery Republican, in the presidential election of 1860. This victory caused South Carolina to secede (separate) from the Union almost immediately. By the time Buchanan left office, in March 1861, six other Southern states had joined South Carolina and formed the Confederacy.

THE FIRST LADY

Buchanan was the only unmarried president. Harriet Lane, his niece, served as White House hostess during his term.

THE VICE-PRESIDENT

John C. Breckenridge of Kentucky was Buchanan's vice-president. In 1860, Southern Democrats nominated him for president. Northern Democrats picked Senator Stephen A. Douglas of Illinois. Both were defeated. When the Southern states seceded, Breckenridge joined them. He became a major general in the Confederate Army.

IN BUCHANAN'S DAY

1858: Minnesota became a state.

1859: Oregon became a state. John Brown attacked an arsenal at Harpers Ferry, Virginia, in an attempt to start a slave revolt. He was captured and hanged.

1860: The Pony Express began service, with relays of riders carrying mail from Missouri to California in just two weeks. The population reached 31 million, including 4 million slaves.

1861: Kansas became a state.

The
Civil War and After (1861–1901)

Just before the dawn on April 12, 1861, Confederate guns opened fire on Fort Sumter, a U.S. Army outpost guarding the harbor at Charleston, South Carolina. The Civil War had begun.

The war was fought over two great issues that had plagued the United States since its founding: slavery and states' rights (the balance of power between the states and the federal government.) The conflict raged for four years and killed more than 600,000 Americans, more than any other U.S. war. One victim was the president who led the country through the war—Abraham Lincoln was assassinated just days after the Confederate surrender.

Fort Sumter, South Carolina, was the scene of the first battle of the Civil War.

When the war was finally over, the slaves were free, and the states that had left the Union to form the Confederacy were won back. North and South began to rebuild. And the United States began to grow again. Industry expanded. Immigrants arrived in waves. Settlers once again headed west, many to start farms on the open plains.

The pioneer days were over by the turn of the century. The last battles had been fought with the Native Americans of the West. The United States was strong and prosperous, and it was ready to take its place as a world power.

1861   Abraham Lincoln is sworn in as president.

The Confederacy is formed; the Civil War begins.

1863   Lincoln issues the Emancipation Proclamation.

Lincoln delivers the Gettysburg Address.

1865   Robert E. Lee surrenders to Ulysses S. Grant; the Civil War ends.

Lincoln is fatally shot shortly after beginning his second term; Andrew Johnson is sworn in as president.

1868   The House of Representatives votes to impeach Johnson.

Ulysses S. Grant wins the presidential election.

1869   The first transcontinental railroad is completed.

1876   Rutherford B. Hayes is elected president.

1880   James A. Garfield is elected president.

1881   Garfield is assassinated. Chester A. Arthur is sworn in as president.

1884   Grover Cleveland is elected president.

1888   Benjamin Harrison is elected president.

1892   Cleveland is elected president again.

1896   William McKinley is elected president.

1898   The Spanish-American War is fought.

1901   McKinley is assassinated.

ABRAHAM LINCOLN

THE 16TH PRESIDENT (1861-1865)

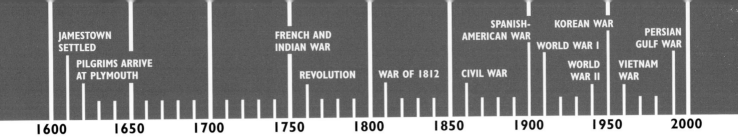
JAMESTOWN SETTLED   FRENCH AND INDIAN WAR   SPANISH-AMERICAN WAR   KOREAN WAR   PERSIAN GULF WAR

PILGRIMS ARRIVE AT PLYMOUTH   REVOLUTION   WAR OF 1812   CIVIL WAR   WORLD WAR I   WORLD WAR II   VIETNAM WAR

1600   1650   1700   1750   1800   1850   1900   1950   2000

- **Born:** February 12, 1809, near Hodgenville, Kentucky
- **Education:** Self-taught; studied law privately
- **Occupation:** Lawyer
- **Political Party:** Republican
- **Vice-Presidents:** Hannibal Hamlin and Andrew Johnson
- **Married:** November 4, 1842, to Mary Todd
- **Children:** Robert, Edward, William ("Willie"), and Thomas ("Tad"); only Robert lived to adulthood
- **Died:** April 15, 1865

Abraham Lincoln's leadership held the North together through the dark years of the Civil War. In his own day, Lincoln was loved by his supporters—and hated by his enemies. But even his critics agreed that he was honest and that his dedication to the Union was unshakable.

Lincoln was the first president born outside the original 13 states. He grew up on the frontier—in Kentucky, Indiana, and Illinois—where life was hard. He was handling an ax by the age of seven, helping his father clear land. Later, he earned money by splitting fence rails for neighbors. Lincoln probably attended school less than a year in all. But he was an eager reader who would travel miles to borrow books.

As a young man, Lincoln worked as a ferryman, a handyman, a shopkeeper, a surveyor, and a postmaster. He was elected to the Illinois legislature; he studied and practiced law in Springfield, Illinois; he served a term in Congress; and he ran unsuccessfully for the Senate.

People got to know this tall, gangly man, and they liked him. His clothes fit poorly, and his manners were not fancy. But Lincoln inspired trust, and he always had a kind word or a funny story. In 1860, the Republicans chose him as their presidential candidate. He won the election.

Within six weeks of his inauguration, North and South were at war. The Union Army was unprepared, and the early battles went against it. As commander-in-chief, President Lincoln rebuilt the army and found generals to lead it. Some of the steps he took were unpopular. For example, men were drafted into (required to serve in) the army. But most people supported him, and the war gradually began to go in the North's favor.

Just weeks after Lincoln began his second term, the war ended, with the surrender of the main Confederate army. Lincoln looked forward to rebuilding the South. But five days later, he was fatally shot by John Wilkes Booth, a supporter of the South, at Ford's Theatre in Washington, D.C.

An 1860 campaign piece.

Lincoln became nationally known during his debates with Douglas.

THE LINCOLN-DOUGLAS DEBATES

In 1858, Abraham Lincoln ran for the U.S. Senate and faced his opponent, Stephen A. Douglas, in a series of debates. Tensions over slavery were mounting. Douglas believed that citizens in each territory should decide the slavery issue for themselves. Lincoln believed that the Union would not survive with some states free and some not: "A house divided against itself cannot stand," he said. He narrowly lost the senatorial election to Douglas. But their debates drew national attention and made Lincoln the best-known Republican in the country.

IN LINCOLN'S WORDS

Abraham Lincoln was a powerful speaker. His most famous speech is the Gettysburg Address, delivered on November 19, 1863, to dedicate a battlefield

Lincoln on a Union Army headquarters inspection, October 1, 1862.

cemetery in Pennsylvania. An old story says that this short speech was quickly jotted on the back of an envelope; but in fact, it was carefully prepared. It contains Lincoln's most famous declaration—that "government of the people, by the people, for the people, shall not perish from the earth."

Lincoln's 1865 inaugural speech is nearly as famous. In it, he called for "malice toward none" and asked the nation's people to "bind up the nation's wounds…and do all which may achieve and cherish a just and lasting peace."

LINCOLN AND SLAVERY

In the years leading up to the Civil War, some Americans worked hard to end slavery everywhere in the United States. Abraham Lincoln opposed slavery throughout his career. But at first, like many leaders of his day, he believed that government could not end slavery where it already existed. He thought that if slavery could be kept out of new territories, it would slowly die.

Lincoln's view changed during the war. He realized that saving the Union was not a great enough cause to rally the North and bring support from the rest of the world. Ending slavery, though, was just such a cause. On January 1, 1863, Lincoln issued the Emancipation Proclamation, in which he proclaimed the emancipation (freedom) of all slaves in the Confederacy.

Because the North and South were still at war, the proclamation could not be enforced. So it did not free any slaves right away. But it did encourage thousands of slaves to escape to freedom in the North. That weakened the South. And, as Lincoln had hoped, the proclamation won support for the North. It also laid the groundwork for the 13th Amendment to the Constitution, which ended slavery throughout the United States.

THE FIRST LADY

Mary Todd Lincoln was a high-spirited young woman from a leading Kentucky family when she married Abraham Lincoln. They were opposites in many ways, but they loved each other deeply. Tragedy marked her years as First Lady. Her son Willie died in 1862, and Mary was at her husband's side when he was shot.

THE VICE-PRESIDENTS

Hannibal Hamlin was Abraham Lincoln's first vice-president. Once a senator from Maine, Hamlin was known for his strong opposition to slavery. Lincoln did not meet Hamlin until after he was nominated, and they often disagreed.

Andrew Johnson was elected vice-president in 1864. Though his roots were in the South, in North Carolina and Tennessee, he remained loyal to the Union.

IN LINCOLN'S DAY

1861: Telegraph lines linked New York City and San Francisco, California.
1862: The Homestead Act offered settlers 160 acres each of free land.
1863: West Virginia became a state.
1864: Nevada became a state.

ANDREW JOHNSON

THE 17TH PRESIDENT (1865-1869)

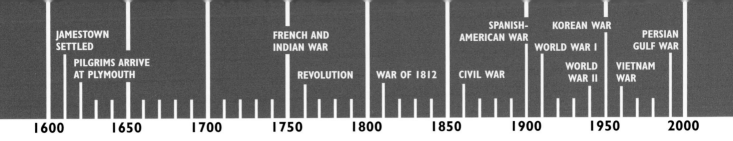

JAMESTOWN SETTLED

PILGRIMS ARRIVE AT PLYMOUTH

FRENCH AND INDIAN WAR

REVOLUTION

WAR OF 1812

SPANISH-AMERICAN WAR

CIVIL WAR

KOREAN WAR

WORLD WAR I

WORLD WAR II

VIETNAM WAR

PERSIAN GULF WAR

1600   1650   1700   1750   1800   1850   1900   1950   2000

- **Born:** December 29, 1808, in Raleigh, North Carolina
- **Education:** Self-taught
- **Occupation:** Tailor
- **Political Party:** Democratic
- **Vice-President:** None
- **Married:** May 17, 1827, to Eliza McCardle
- **Children:** Martha, Charles, Mary, Robert, and Andrew
- **Died:** July 31, 1875

Abraham Lincoln's vice-president, Andrew Johnson, was sworn in as president the same day that Lincoln died; thus, he did not have a vice-president. Johnson was determined to follow Lincoln's plan for a "just and lasting peace." But he battled so strongly with Congress that he was nearly tossed out of office.

A tailor from Tennessee, Johnson had opposed slavery. Still, he believed that forgiveness was the best policy for Reconstruction (the rebuilding of the South). But many in Congress thought that Johnson was much too easy on the South. Congress refused to seat representatives from Southern states until the rights of freed slaves were guaranteed. Then it set aside the Southern governments that Johnson had set up, putting the army in control of the South.

An admission ticket to the impeachment trial.

By 1868, disagreement between Congress and the president was so fierce that the House of Representatives voted to impeach him—that is, charge him with misconduct. If found guilty, Johnson would be removed from office. Johnson was tried in the Senate. This was the first such trial in U.S. history, and spectators filled the Senate gallery. Johnson was acquitted (cleared of the charges) by one vote.

THE FIRST LADY

Eliza McCardle Johnson, a shoemaker's daughter, was 16 when she married Andrew Johnson. She taught him writing and arithmetic and encouraged him to study. As First Lady, she often left the duties of White House hostess to her oldest daughter, Martha Johnson Patterson.

IN JOHNSON'S DAY

1865: The 13th Amendment was ratified, abolishing slavery.

1866: The first successful transatlantic telegraph cable linked the United States and Britain.

1867: The United States purchased Alaska from Russia for $7.2 million—about two cents an acre. Nebraska became a state.

1868: The 14th Amendment was ratified, guaranteeing citizenship to former slaves. The Treaty of Fort Laramie ended two years of fighting on the Great Plains between the army and the Sioux (Lakota), under the leadership of Red Cloud.

ULYSSES S. GRANT

THE 18TH PRESIDENT (1869-1877)

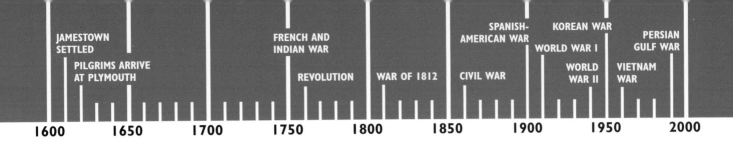

JAMESTOWN SETTLED		FRENCH AND INDIAN WAR			SPANISH-AMERICAN WAR	KOREAN WAR		PERSIAN GULF WAR
	PILGRIMS ARRIVE AT PLYMOUTH		REVOLUTION	WAR OF 1812		WORLD WAR I		
					CIVIL WAR		WORLD WAR II	VIETNAM WAR

1600   1650   1700   1750   1800   1850   1900   1950   2000

- **Born:** April 27, 1822, in Point Pleasant, Ohio
- **Education:** Graduated from the U.S. Military Academy in 1843
- **Occupation:** Soldier
- **Political Party:** Republican
- **Vice-Presidents:** Schuyler Colfax and Henry Wilson
- **Married:** August 22, 1848, to Julia Dent
- **Children:** Frederick, Ulysses, Ellen ("Nellie"), and Jesse
- **Died:** July 23, 1885

Ulysses Simpson Grant gained fame as the general who led the Union to victory in the Civil War. He was a better soldier than politician. Grant was not a very strong president, and his two terms were marked by scandal.

During the war, Grant showed his skill with a string of victories. He was promoted and was eventually put in charge of all the Union armies. When he received the surrender of Confederate general Robert E. Lee in 1865, Grant became a national hero. He easily won election as president in 1868. But he had little idea of what the job would involve and no real plan for the country.

Rather than picking the most qualified people, Grant appointed his friends and supporters to hold important government jobs. Some of these people were not trustworthy and were later charged with fraud and corruption. Grand was not involved in their schemes, but he was discredited by these scandals. Still, he remained popular and respected for his military skill.

Late in life, Grant lost all his money in various investment and business failures. He provided for his family by writing his memoirs. The book became a huge best-seller.

THE FIRST LADY

Julia Dent Grant was the sister of one of Ulysses S. Grant's West Point classmates. At the White House, she entertained elegantly. In 1874, the White House wedding of the Grants' daughter, Nellie, was typically lavish, with the East Room of the mansion awash in white roses.

THE VICE-PRESIDENTS

Schuyler Colfax of Indiana was vice-president during Grant's first term. He had been speaker (leader) of the House of Representatives. In 1872, he was accused of taking bribes from railroad officials.

Henry Wilson, a senator from Massachusetts, was vice-president during Grant's second term. Like Colfax, Wilson was said to be involved in scandals.

IN GRANT'S DAY

1869: The first transcontinental railroad was completed.

1870: The U.S. population neared 40 million. A huge fire swept through Chicago, destroying much of the city.

1876: Alexander Graham Bell invented the telephone.

RUTHERFORD B. HAYES

THE 19TH PRESIDENT (1877-1881)

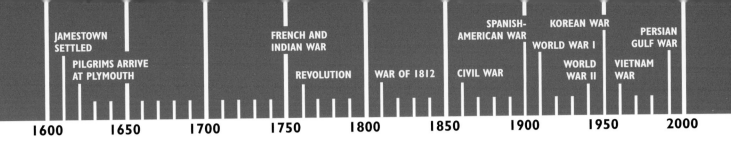

| JAMESTOWN SETTLED | PILGRIMS ARRIVE AT PLYMOUTH | FRENCH AND INDIAN WAR | REVOLUTION | WAR OF 1812 | CIVIL WAR | SPANISH-AMERICAN WAR | WORLD WAR I | KOREAN WAR | WORLD WAR II | VIETNAM WAR | PERSIAN GULF WAR |

| 1600 | 1650 | 1700 | 1750 | 1800 | 1850 | 1900 | 1950 | 2000 |

- **Born:** October 4, 1822, in Delaware, Ohio
- **Education:** Graduated from Harvard Law School in 1845
- **Occupation:** Lawyer
- **Political Party:** Republican
- **Vice-President:** William A. Wheeler
- **Married:** December 30, 1852, to Lucy Ware Webb
- **Children:** Birchard, James, Rutherford, Fanny, and Scott; three other sons died in early childhood
- **Died:** January 17, 1893

Rutherford Birchard Hayes is as well known for the way he came to the presidency as for anything he did in office. In 1876, Hayes, the Republican governor of Ohio, ran for president against Samuel J. Tilden, the Democratic governor of New York. Tilden actually won more popular votes than Hayes. But some electoral votes were challenged, and both political parties were charged with using threats and fraud to win votes. The election was deadlocked.

A special commission was appointed to review the votes, and it ruled in favor of Hayes. Democrats in Congress objected, but they finally agreed to accept him. In exchange, the Republicans informally agreed to end Reconstruction (the rebuilding of the South after the Civil War). They withdrew the army troops that had occupied the South since the war.

Hayes kept that promise and another: to serve only one term. He earned a reputation for honesty as president. One of his goals was to reform the civil service system, so that appointments of government jobs would go to qualified people rather than to friends and relatives of politicians.

THE FIRST LADY

Lucy Ware Webb Hayes was the first First Lady to hold a college degree. She was known for her support of some of the important causes of her day, including the abolition of slavery and the prohibition (banning) of alcohol. Because she refused to serve alcoholic drinks at the White House, she was nicknamed "Lemonade Lucy."

THE VICE-PRESIDENT

William A. Wheeler of served in the House of Representatives before becoming Hayes's vice-president. In 1873, when Congress voted itself a big pay raise, the New York representative refused to profit by it. He used his salary increase to buy government bonds. He then canceled the bonds, so that the money went back to the government.

IN HAYES'S DAY

1877: Chief Joseph of the Nez Percé surrendered after leading a four-month campaign against the U.S. Army in the Northwest.

1878: The first national labor union, the Knights of Labor, met in Philadelphia.

1880: Thomas Edison patented his electric lightbulb. The U.S. population topped 50 million people.

JAMES A. GARFIELD

THE 20TH PRESIDENT (1881)

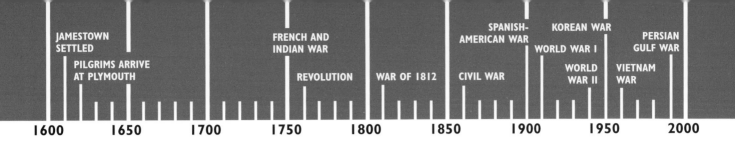

1600	1650	1700	1750	1800	1850	1900	1950	2000

JAMESTOWN SETTLED

PILGRIMS ARRIVE AT PLYMOUTH

FRENCH AND INDIAN WAR

REVOLUTION

WAR OF 1812

CIVIL WAR

SPANISH-AMERICAN WAR

WORLD WAR I

WORLD WAR II

KOREAN WAR

VIETNAM WAR

PERSIAN GULF WAR

- **Born:** November 19, 1831, in Orange, Ohio
- **Education:** Graduated from Williams College in 1856
- **Occupation:** Teacher; soldier
- **Political Party:** Republican
- **Vice-President:** Chester A. Arthur
- **Married:** November 11, 1858, to Lucretia Rudolph
- **Children:** Harry, James, Mary, Irvin, and Abram; another son and daughter died in early childhood
- **Died:** September 19, 1881

James Abram Garfield served only four months as president. On July 2, 1881, he was shot while at a Washington, D.C., railroad station. His assassin, Charles Guiteau, had been angered by the new president's refusal to give him a diplomatic post. Garfield lingered until September 19. But his wounds soon became infected, and in his day there were no antibiotics to cure infection.

Garfield, born in a log cabin, was the son of pioneers. His family was poor, but he managed to get an education, supporting himself by teaching and doing odd jobs. He was a professor and then president of Hiram College in Ohio, and he fought on the side of the Union in the Civil War. Garfield also was elected to eight terms in the House of Representatives. By 1880, when he was elected president, he was an important Republican leader.

Garfield's assassination by a disappointed job-seeker shocked Americans. People realized that the spoils system—through which politicians rewarded their supporters with government jobs—had gotten far out of control. Pressure for reform now grew stronger.

THE FIRST LADY

Lucretia Rudolph Garfield and James Garfield had met while both were students at the school that would later become Hiram College. James Garfield once praised her for meeting "every new emergency with fine tact and faultless taste." She proved that to be true during the weeks before his death, staying at his side despite suffering herself from illness and exhaustion.

THE VICE-PRESIDENT

Chester A. Arthur was reluctant to take over the president's duties while Garfield lay wounded but still living. He had long been a power behind the scenes in the Republican party, but he had not held an elected office before becoming vice-president.

IN GARFIELD'S DAY

1881: The American Red Cross was organized, formed by Civil War nurse Clara Barton. Booker T. Washington started Tuskegee Institute in Alabama, to provide higher education for African Americans.

CHESTER A. ARTHUR

THE 21ST PRESIDENT (1881-1885)

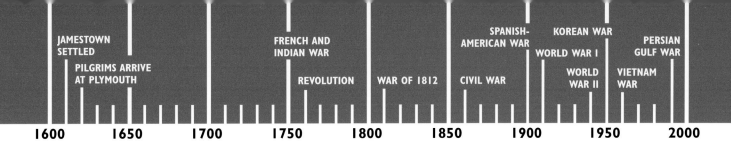

JAMESTOWN SETTLED

PILGRIMS ARRIVE AT PLYMOUTH

FRENCH AND INDIAN WAR

REVOLUTION

WAR OF 1812

CIVIL WAR

SPANISH-AMERICAN WAR

KOREAN WAR

WORLD WAR I

WORLD WAR II

VIETNAM WAR

PERSIAN GULF WAR

1600 1650 1700 1750 1800 1850 1900 1950 2000

- **Born:** October 5, 1829, in North Fairfield, Vermont
- **Education:** Graduated from Union College in 1848
- **Occupation:** Teacher; lawyer
- **Political Party:** Republican
- **Vice-President:** None
- **Married:** October 25, 1859, to Ellen Herndon
- **Children:** Chester, Ellen; another son died in early childhood
- **Died:** November 18, 1886

"Chet Arthur president!" a leading Republican exclaimed when President James A. Garfield died. Like many people, he expected the worst. But Chester Alan Arthur surprised everyone.

In the 1850s, as a New York City lawyer, Arthur had benefited from the spoils system of party politics. His support of Republican politicians won him jobs and favors. And his love of fine living won him the nickname "Gentleman Boss." Arthur ordered suits from London and was especially proud of his mutton-chop whiskers.

In 1877, Arthur was fired as collector of the Port of New York for closing his eyes to corruption. He was still important in the Republican party. But even when the Republicans made him their vice-presidential candidate, no one expected him to become president. And when he was sworn in, everyone thought that the spoils system would guide his administration. (Because Vice-President Arthur succeeded Garfield as president, he did not have his own vice-president.)

But Arthur stood up to the political bosses. He appointed qualified people to government jobs and fought corruption. In the process, he made enemies in his party, and he was not nominated for a second term as president.

THE FIRST LADY

Ellen ("Nell") Herndon Arthur died less than two years before her husband became president. Nell was the daughter of a distinguished Virginia family. While in the White House, Chester Arthur had fresh flowers placed by her photograph every day. His sister, Mary Arthur McElroy, often took on the role of hostess for official functions.

IN ARTHUR'S DAY

1883: The Brooklyn Bridge was completed in New York City; at 1,595 feet, it was then the longest suspension bridge in the world. Frontier scout William F. Cody introduced "Buffalo Bill's Wild West," a show that dramatized the legends of the West.

Dedication of the Brooklyn Bridge.

1884: The first skyscraper, the Home Insurance Building, was built in Chicago, Illinois. Mark Twain's novel *The Adventures of Huckleberry Finn* was published.

GROVER CLEVELAND

THE 22ND AND 24TH PRESIDENT (1885-1889; 1893-1897)

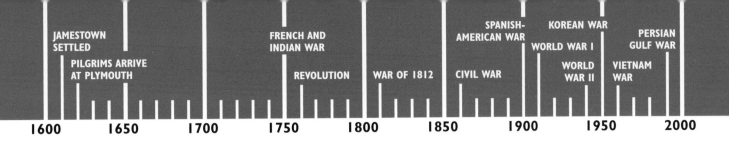

			SPANISH-AMERICAN WAR	KOREAN WAR	PERSIAN
JAMESTOWN SETTLED		FRENCH AND INDIAN WAR		WORLD WAR I	GULF WAR
PILGRIMS ARRIVE AT PLYMOUTH		REVOLUTION	WAR OF 1812	CIVIL WAR	WORLD WAR II	VIETNAM WAR

1600   1650   1700   1750   1800   1850   1900   1950   2000

- **Born:** March 18, 1837, in Caldwell, New Jersey
- **Education:** Studied law privately
- **Occupation:** Lawyer
- **Political Party:** Democratic
- **Vice-Presidents:** Thomas A. Hendricks and Adlai Stevenson
- **Married:** June 2, 1886, to Frances Folsom
- **Children:** Esther, Marion, Richard, and Francis; another daughter died in early childhood
- **Died:** June 24, 1908

Grover Cleveland was the only U.S. president to serve two terms that were not consecutive (back to back). In both, he earned a reputation for honesty and firmness. Cleveland was a large, jovial man whose family called him Uncle Jumbo. He always tried to do the right thing, even when it made him unpopular.

Cleveland practiced law for many years in Buffalo, New York, before entering politics. In 1881, he was elected mayor of that city. He did such a good job of reforming the city's corrupt government that he was elected governor of New York the next year. His reputation spread further. Just three years after entering politics, he became president—the first Democrat in that post in 24 years. He lost the election of 1888, but he was reelected in 1892.

In office, Cleveland worked to weed out corruption and waste. He also sought to lower tariffs (taxes on imported goods), and he opposed labor strikes. He worked long hours and sometimes even answered the White House telephone himself. Some of his actions were not popular, and he was blamed for an economic slump in his second term. But many historians now consider him one of the best American presidents.

THE FIRST LADY

Frances ("Frank") Folsom Cleveland was 21 when she married Grover Cleveland in 1886. It was the first time that a president was married in the White House. Frank was the daughter of Cleveland's former law partner.

THE VICE-PRESIDENTS

Thomas A. Hendricks was the vice-president during Cleveland's first term. He had been governor of Indiana.

Adlai Stevenson of Illinois was the vice-president during Cleveland's second term. Previously, he had served in Congress.

IN CLEVELAND'S DAY

1886:   The Statue of Liberty was dedicated in New York City. Apache leader Geronimo surrendered to the army in Arizona.

1888:   A blizzard blanketed the East Coast, killing 400 people.

1893:   Charles and J. Frank Duryea build the first gasoline-powered automobile in America.

1894:   Government troops broke up the Pullman strike, which had halted railroad traffic.

1896:   Utah became a state.

BENJAMIN HARRISON

THE 23RD PRESIDENT (1889-1893)

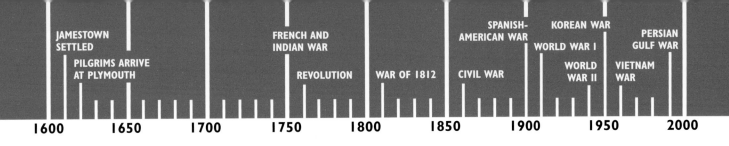

1600	1650	1700	1750	1800	1850	1900	1950	2000

JAMESTOWN SETTLED

PILGRIMS ARRIVE AT PLYMOUTH

FRENCH AND INDIAN WAR

REVOLUTION

WAR OF 1812

CIVIL WAR

SPANISH-AMERICAN WAR

KOREAN WAR

WORLD WAR I

WORLD WAR II

VIETNAM WAR

PERSIAN GULF WAR

- **Born:** August 20, 1833, in North Bend, Ohio
- **Education:** Graduated from Miami University (Ohio) in 1852
- **Occupation:** Lawyer
- **Political Party:** Republican
- **Vice-President:** Levi P. Morton
- **Married:** October 20, 1853, to Caroline Scott; April 6, 1896, to Mary Scott Lord
- **Children:** Russell, Mary, and Elizabeth
- **Died:** March 13, 1901

Benjamin Harrison's family played a leading role in American history. His great-grandfather, also named Benjamin, was one of the signers of the Declaration of Independence. His grandfather, William Henry Harrison, was the ninth president. And his father, John Scott Harrison, was a congressman. It was not surprising then, that Benjamin Harrison would have an interest in politics.

Harrison ignored his father's warning that only "knaves" (dishonest men) entered politics. A successful lawyer who had fought in the Civil War, he was elected to the Senate in 1880. Then, in 1888, Harrison ran for president. He did not go on the campaign trail, however. He stayed at his home in Indiana and delivered off-the-cuff speeches to visitors. This "front-porch campaign" brought him fewer popular votes than his opponent, Grover Cleveland. But he won the electoral vote, and so he became president.

Harrison believed that the United States could play a bigger role in world affairs, and he focused on foreign policy. He also supported efforts to break up trusts—big business monopolies. Harrison was respected for his intelligence and independence, but he did not win a second term.

THE FIRST LADY

Caroline Scott Harrison took a special interest in history as First Lady. But in October 1892, she died at the White House of tuberculosis. When her husband lost his bid for reelection a few weeks later, he said that the defeat had "no sting" in comparison to this loss. Benjamin Harrison later married Mary Scott Lord Dimmick, a relative of his first wife's.

THE VICE-PRESIDENT

Levi P. Morton, Harrison's vice-president, was a New York banker. He had been a strong supporter of the Republican party but had no government experience. He later became governor of New York.

IN HARRISON'S DAY

1889: Native-American land in Oklahoma was opened to white settlers, setting off the first of several land rushes. At Johnstown, Pennsylvania, the collapse of a dam led to a flood that killed 2,000 people. Montana, North Dakota, South Dakota, and Washington became states.

1890: More than half a million immigrants arrived, bringing the U.S. population to nearly 63 million. Idaho and Wyoming became states. At Wounded Knee, South Dakota, U.S. troops killed more than 100 Sioux (Lakota), many of whom were women and children.

WILLIAM McKINLEY

THE 25TH PRESIDENT (1897-1901)

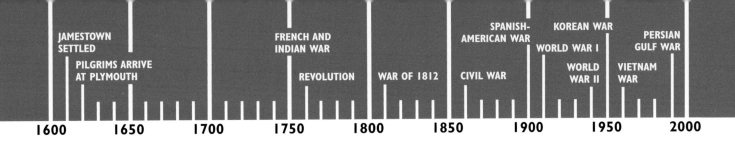

| JAMESTOWN SETTLED | | FRENCH AND INDIAN WAR | | | | SPANISH-AMERICAN WAR | KOREAN WAR | PERSIAN GULF WAR |
| PILGRIMS ARRIVE AT PLYMOUTH | | REVOLUTION | WAR OF 1812 | CIVIL WAR | | | WORLD WAR I | WORLD WAR II | VIETNAM WAR |

| 1600 | 1650 | 1700 | 1750 | 1800 | 1850 | 1900 | 1950 | 2000 |

- **Born:** January 29, 1843
- **Education:** Allegheny College (1860-1861)
- **Occupation:** Lawyer
- **Political Party:** Republican
- **Vice-Presidents:** Garret A. Hobart and Theodore Roosevelt
- **Married:** January 25, 1871, to Ida Sacton
- **Children:** Katherine and Ida; both died in early childhood
- **Died:** September 14, 1901

When William McKinley became president, war fever was growing in the United States. The cause was the island of Cuba, where people were rebelling against Spanish rule. Many Americans wanted the United States to step in on the side of the rebels. Then, in 1898, the U.S. warship *Maine* mysteriously blew up while visiting Cuba. As a result, McKinley asked Congress to declare war on Spain.

The Spanish-American War lasted just 113 days. Cuba won independence from Spain, and the United States won new territories—Puerto Rico, Guam, and the Philippine Islands. Some Americans were against keeping these territories, arguing that a democratic country should not build an empire. But McKinley approved. Most voters agreed with him; he easily won a second term.

In September 1901, McKinley delivered an important speech at the Pan-American Exposition held in Buffalo, New York. The next day, at a public reception, he was shot by Leon Czolgosz, an anarchist (a person opposed to all government). McKinley died eight days later, the third American president to be assassinated.

THE FIRST LADY

Ida Sacton McKinley was a well-educated, well-traveled, lively young woman when she married William McKinley. But epilepsy and other illnesses had caused her to be largely bedridden by the time she became First Lady. She received guests seated, and her husband was always at her side to help her.

THE VICE-PRESIDENTS

Garret A. Hobart, a state senator from New Jersey, was vice-president during McKinley's first term. A close friend of the president, he died while in office.

During McKinley's second term, Theodore Roosevelt was vice-president. He was a hero of the Spanish-American War and governor of New York. When McKinley was shot, Roosevelt was on vacation in the Adirondack Mountains. He rushed to Buffalo, arriving after the president died.

IN McKINLEY'S DAY

1897: Prospectors swarmed to Alaska by the thousands in search of gold.
1898: The United States annexed Hawaii.
1900: The U.S. population neared 76 million.

The Twentieth Century

*B*y the start of the twentieth century, the United States had gained practically all the territory it would hold. The country kept growing—but in other ways than in land. Now, thousands of immigrants arrived, from all parts of the world. They helped make the country an industrial leader. And the United States began to play a bigger role in world affairs.

These changes brought much good, but the United States also had problems. In the first half of the century, the country fought two world wars. In between the wars, it went from good times to hard times—from the booming Roaring Twenties to the devastating economic depression of the

New immigrants arrive at Ellis Island Immigrant Building, in New York Harbor.

1930s. Much of the second half of the century was taken up with the Cold War. This long-lasting rivalry between the Soviet Union and other Communist nations on the one hand, and the United States and other democratic nations on the other, lasted until 1990. And Americans struggled with serious social problems, especially race relations and poverty.

The presidents who led the country through these times had to meet new challenges. Among them were strong leaders who expanded the role of the presidency. More than ever, the president became the person who Americans looked to in times of trouble.

1901 Theodore Roosevelt is sworn in as president.

1908 William Howard Taft is elected president.

1912 Woodrow Wilson is elected president.

1917 The United States enters World War I.

1918 Germany surrenders and World War I ends.

1920 Warren G. Harding is elected president.

1923 Harding dies while in office. Calvin Coolidge is sworn in as president.

1928 Herbert Hoover wins the presidential election.

1929 The Great Depression begins.

1932 Franklin D. Roosevelt is elected president.

1941 Japan bombs Pearl Harbor; the United States enters World War II.

1944 Roosevelt wins an unprecedented fourth term.

1945 Roosevelt dies of a stroke; Harry S. Truman is sworn in as president.
World War II ends.

1950 The Korean War begins.

1952 Dwight D. Eisenhower is elected president.

1953 The Korean War ends.

1960 John F. Kennedy is elected president.

1963 Kennedy is assassinated; Lyndon B. Johnson is sworn in as president.
U.S. buildup in Vietnam begins.

1968 Richard M. Nixon is elected president.

1973 U. S. soldiers leave Vietnam.

1974 Nixon resigns to avoid impeachment; Gerald R. Ford is sworn in as president.

1976 James E. Carter is elected president.

1980 Ronald Reagan is elected president.

1983 Reagan sends troops to Grenada.

1988 George Bush is elected president.

1991 The Persian Gulf War is fought.

1992 William J. Clinton wins presidential election.

THEODORE ROOSEVELT

THE 26TH PRESIDENT (1901-1909)

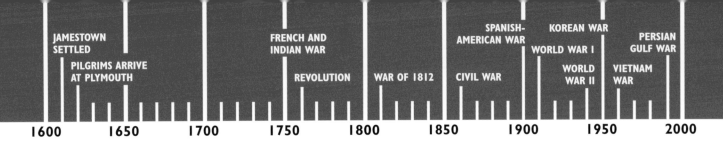

| JAMESTOWN SETTLED | | FRENCH AND INDIAN WAR | | | SPANISH-AMERICAN WAR | KOREAN WAR | | PERSIAN GULF WAR |
| | PILGRIMS ARRIVE AT PLYMOUTH | | REVOLUTION | WAR OF 1812 | CIVIL WAR | WORLD WAR I | WORLD WAR II | VIETNAM WAR |

1600   1650   1700   1750   1800   1850   1900   1950   2000

- **Born:** October 27, 1858, in New York City
- **Education:** Graduated from Harvard University in 1880
- **Occupation:** Writer
- **Political Party:** Republican
- **Vice-President:** Charles W. Fairbanks
- **Married:** October 27, 1880, to Alice Hathaway Lee
  December 26, 1886, to Edith Carow
- **Children:** Alice, Theodore, Kermit, Ethel, Archibald, and Quentin
- **Died:** January 6, 1919

Teddy Roosevelt (center) with the Rough Riders.

When Theodore Roosevelt became president, he was 42—the youngest person ever to hold the office. TR, or Teddy, as he was called, was one of the most popular presidents. He had boundless enthusiasm for everything from hunting to literature. And he used the presidency to help improve life for Americans.

Roosevelt nearly turned his back on politics early in his career. In 1884, his first wife, Alice Lee Roosevelt, and his mother died on the same day. Grief-stricken, Roosevelt went west. For two years, he raised cattle in the Dakotas. But his cattle business failed. He returned to New York and a series of government jobs.

Roosevelt was assistant secretary of the U.S. Navy when the Spanish-American War broke out in 1898. He signed up to command a cavalry regiment, which became known as the Rough Riders. In Cuba, he led this unit on a charge against Spanish positions on Kettle Hill. The action, misnamed "The Charge of San Juan Hill," made Roosevelt famous. It helped him win election as governor of New York, and then as vice-president under McKinley.

When McKinley was assassinated, Roosevelt promised to continue his policies. But he soon put his own stamp on the presidency, and he won the election of 1904 by a huge margin. Roosevelt believed that average Americans deserved a "square deal," and he often sided with them against the rich. He took steps to control and even break up trusts, the business monopolies that controlled the railroads and other industries. He pressed for laws to protect people from unsafe working conditions and impure foods and drugs. He opposed racial discrimination.

One of Roosevelt's favorite proverbs was "Speak softly and carry a big stick." Some of his actions toward other countries were termed "big-stick diplomacy." For example, he sent the American fleet on a worldwide cruise to show its strength. And he took the view that the United States, to protect its interests, could step into the affairs of Latin American countries. Thus, the United States got involved in Panama and the Dominican Republic.

But Roosevelt avoided war and worked hard to keep up friendly relations abroad. He won the Nobel Peace Prize in 1906 for negotiating an end to a war between Japan and Russia.

ROOSEVELT AND CONSERVATION

Theodore Roosevelt was one of the finest naturalists of his time; he had a deep and abiding appreciation for the natural world. And he was one of few who realized that what was left of the American wilderness would disappear if it fell into the hands of private developers. He believed that the wilderness and the resources it contained, including timber from the forests and the minerals under the ground, should be preserved for the use and enjoyment of future generations.

To do that, Roosevelt reorganized the federal Forest Service. He staffed the agency with trained foresters and tripled the amount of forest land protected in reserves. He also persuaded timber companies to cut trees selectively, so that less forested land would be stripped. He placed new controls on mining. And he doubled the number of national parks by creating five, including Crater Lake in Oregon. Sixteen wild areas, such as Muir Woods in California, were made national monuments, and more than 50 others became wildlife refuges.

President Roosevelt poses in front of the Grizzly Giant, the redwood that is the biggest tree in California.

After Roosevelt left office, he went on a year-long African safari. When he returned to the United States, he reentered politics. He broke with the leaders of the Republican party, saying that they favored the rich. In 1912, he ran for president on the Progressive, or Bull Moose, ticket. He lost, but he continued to speak out on the issues of the day.

THE PANAMA CANAL

While he was president, Theodore Roosevelt set in motion a plan to build a shipping canal through the narrow Isthmus of Panama, in Central America. At that time, ships traveling from the East Coast to the West Coast of the United States had to go all the way around the tip of South America, a trip that took months. Roosevelt knew that a canal would benefit the United States by shortening the journey. But Colombia, which controlled the isthmus, rejected

his plan for a canal. Roosevelt then supported a revolution in Panama. Once independent, Panama granted the United States rights to a strip of land across the isthmus. Roosevelt went there to see the building of the canal, which was not finished until after he left office.

This political cartoon expressed approval of Roosevelt's run for the presidency in 1912.

THE FIRST LADY

Edith Carow Roosevelt had been a childhood playmate of TR's. They married two years after the death of his first wife, Alice Hathaway Lee, and he came to rely on Edith's advice and judgment. The White House was a lively place during her time there. Six children and dozens of pets, including a pony and snakes, were in residence.

THE VICE-PRESIDENT

Charles W. Fairbanks, a senator from Indiana, was elected with Roosevelt in 1904. He hoped to be president after him. But the two often disagreed. In the 1908 campaign, Roosevelt gave his support to William Howard Taft instead.

IN ROOSEVELT'S DAY

1903: Orville and Wilbur Wright made the first successful airplane flight, at Kitty Hawk, North Carolina.

1906: Much of San Francisco was destroyed in a major earthquake and fire.

1907: Oklahoma became a state.

1908: Henry Ford introduced the Model T car.

WILLIAM H. TAFT

THE 27TH PRESIDENT (1909-1913)

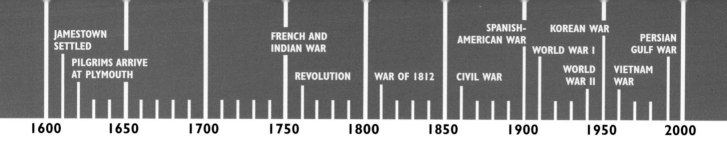

1600	1650	1700	1750	1800	1850	1900	1950	2000

- **Born:** September 15, 1857, in Cincinnati, Ohio
- **Education:** Graduated from Yale College in 1878 and from Cincinnati Law School in 1880
- **Occupation:** Lawyer; judge
- **Political Party:** Republican
- **Vice-President:** James S. Sherman
- **Married:** June 19, 1886, to Helen Herron
- **Children:** Robert, Helen, and Charles
- **Died:** March 8, 1930

"Politics, when I am in it, makes me sick," William Howard Taft wrote in 1906. Taft had no wish to run for president. But two years later, at the urging of his family and his friend Theodore Roosevelt, he did, and was elected.

A large man (he weighed more than 300 pounds), Taft had been a respected lawyer and judge. In 1901, he became governor of the newly acquired Philippine Islands and moved that territory toward self-government. He then served as Roosevelt's secretary of war. When he succeeded (followed) Roosevelt as president, he continued many of TR's policies.

However, Theodore Roosevelt felt that his old friend was too conservative and favored the rich. So in 1912, he challenged Taft for the Republican nomination. When Taft won the nomination, Roosevelt ran as an Independent. In the election, Republicans divided their votes between the two men, and the Democrats won.

Taft's career was not over, though. Nine years later, he reached one of his great goals: He was appointed chief justice of the U.S. Supreme Court. Taft preferred that job to the presidency, and many historians believe that he was better at it.

THE FIRST LADY

Helen Herron Taft took an interest in politics and her husband's career. As First Lady, she presided over glittering social events. The Tafts were the last family to keep a cow at the White House, and the first to keep a car. Washington's famous cherry trees were planted around the Tidal Basin at Helen Taft's request.

THE VICE-PRESIDENT

James S. Sherman had been a congressman from New York. He was on the Taft ticket in 1912, too, but he died during the campaign. It was too late to replace him on the ballot, and about 3 million Americans cast votes for him anyway.

IN TAFT'S DAY

1909: Explorers Robert Peary and Matthew Henson reached the North Pole.
1910: The U.S. population was 92 million.
1911: A fire at the Triangle Shirtwaist Factory in New York City killed 146 workers, drawing attention to unsafe factories.
1912: New Mexico and Arizona became states. Some 1,500 people, including many Americans, died when the British ocean liner *Titanic* sank in the North Atlantic.

WOODROW WILSON

THE 28TH PRESIDENT (1913-1921)

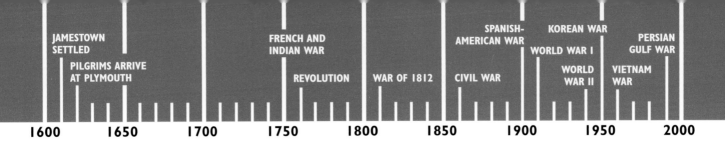

| JAMESTOWN SETTLED | | FRENCH AND INDIAN WAR | | | SPANISH-AMERICAN WAR | KOREAN WAR | PERSIAN GULF WAR |
| PILGRIMS ARRIVE AT PLYMOUTH | | REVOLUTION | WAR OF 1812 | CIVIL WAR | WORLD WAR I | WORLD WAR II | VIETNAM WAR |

1600   1650   1700   1750   1800   1850   1900   1950   2000

- **Born:** December 28, 1856, in Staunton, Virginia
- **Education:** Graduated from the College of New Jersey (present-day Princeton University) in 1879; received a doctorate from Johns Hopkins University in 1886
- **Occupation:** Professor; public official
- **Political Party:** Democratic
- **Vice-President:** Thomas R. Marshall
- **Married:** June 24, 1885, to Ellen Axson; December 18, 1915, to Edith Bolling Galt
- **Children:** Margaret, Jesse, and Eleanor
- **Died:** February 3, 1924

Woodrow Wilson grew up in the South during the Civil War. He never forgot the experience. When he was president, he led the United States through World War I. He then worked to found the League of Nations (later to become the United Nations), which he hoped would prevent future wars.

Wilson was a respected scholar before he entered politics. As a professor and the president of Princeton University, he became known for his educational reforms. Later, as governor of New Jersey, he became even more well known for his reforms of government. The reputation helped Wilson to win the presidency.

World War I broke out in Europe in 1914. At first, Americans hoped to stay out of it. But in 1917, after German submarines attacked U.S. ships, President Wilson asked Congress to declare war. While U.S. soldiers fought overseas, Wilson set out "Fourteen Points" as a basis for peace. After Germany surrendered in 1918, he helped draw up a peace treaty that provided for the League of Nations. He won the 1919 Nobel Peace Prize for this. But to his disappointment, Congress refused to bring the United States into the League.

THE FIRST LADIES

Woodrow Wilson's first wife, Ellen Axson Wilson, daughter of a Georgia clergyman, tried to maintain her family's privacy as much as possible in the White House. She fell ill and died in 1914.

Edith Bolling Galt Wilson, the president's second wife, was a great support. In October 1920, Woodrow Wilson suffered a stroke, and he was largely bedridden for the rest of his term. She managed his appointments and even guided his hand when he had to sign papers.

THE VICE-PRESIDENT

Thomas R. Marshall, a former governor of Indiana, refused to declare himself president when Wilson fell ill. He is famous for the saying, "What this country needs is a good five-cent cigar."

IN WILSON'S DAY

1915: Telephone lines linked New York City and San Francisco, California.

1916: U.S. troops were ordered into Mexico in pursuit of Pancho Villa, who had raided American towns.

1919: Prohibition began as the 18th Amendment banned alcohol in the United States.

1920: The 19th Amendment granted women the right to vote. The U.S. population was 106 million.

WARREN G. HARDING

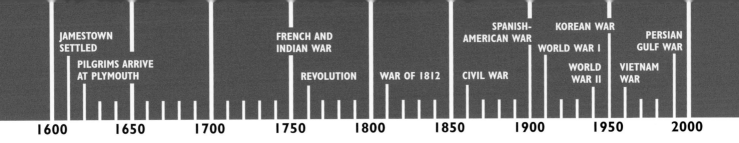

| 1600 | 1650 | 1700 | 1750 | 1800 | 1850 | 1900 | 1950 | 2000 |

JAMESTOWN SETTLED

PILGRIMS ARRIVE AT PLYMOUTH

FRENCH AND INDIAN WAR

REVOLUTION

WAR OF 1812

CIVIL WAR

SPANISH-AMERICAN WAR

KOREAN WAR

WORLD WAR I

WORLD WAR II

VIETNAM WAR

PERSIAN GULF WAR

- **Born:** November 2, 1865
- **Education:** Graduated from Ohio Central College in 1882
- **Occupation:** Newspaper publisher
- **Political Party:** Republican
- **Vice-President:** Calvin Coolidge
- **Married:** July 8, 1891, to Florence Kling
- **Children:** None
- **Died:** August 2, 1923

Warren Gamaliel Harding once said that his goal was to be America's best-loved president. Instead, he is one of the least known of the presidents. He died after only two and a half years in office, having accomplished little. And after his death, reports of scandal and corruption at high levels in his administration ruined his reputation.

Harding was a likable, attractive man who had been a successful small-town newspaper publisher. A good speaker, he had served in the Senate. He had an easygoing style as president, and some people took advantage of this. Although President Harding was honest, some of those who worked under him were not. Scandals began to break out, especially after he fell ill and died in August 1923.

The worst case of corruption to occur during Harding's presidency was the Teapot Dome Scandal. It was called this because it involved misuse of government land in California and at Teapot Dome, Wyoming. Harding's secretary of the Interior, Albert Fall, was found to have taken bribes from oil company executives. In exchange, he let them drill for oil on the land, even though the oil there was supposed to be reserved for the navy.

THE FIRST LADY

Florence Kling Harding's drive and determination contributed to her husband's success. She ran the circulation department of his newspaper and helped it make money. She worked hard for his election. And as First Lady, she kept up with a crowded calendar of social events.

THE VICE-PRESIDENT

Calvin Coolidge was the first vice-president to attend cabinet meetings regularly. He was visiting his father's house in Vermont when he was awakened in the early hours of August 3, 1923, with the news of Warren G. Harding's death. He got up, went downstairs to the dining room, and was sworn in as president by his father, a notary public. Then he went back to bed.

IN HARDING'S DAY

1921: Congress passed the Quota Act, which limited immigration.

1922: A coal-mine strike in Illinois erupted in violence, leaving 36 people dead. The Lincoln Memorial was dedicated in Washington, D.C.

CALVIN COOLIDGE

THE 30TH PRESIDENT (1923-1929)

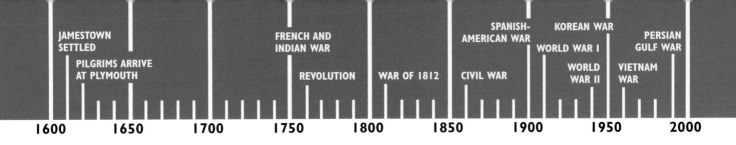

JAMESTOWN SETTLED

PILGRIMS ARRIVE AT PLYMOUTH

FRENCH AND INDIAN WAR

REVOLUTION

WAR OF 1812

SPANISH-AMERICAN WAR

CIVIL WAR

KOREAN WAR

WORLD WAR I

WORLD WAR II

VIETNAM WAR

PERSIAN GULF WAR

1600   1650   1700   1750   1800   1850   1900   1950   2000

- **Born:** July 4, 1872, in Plymouth Notch, Vermont
- **Education:** Graduated from Amherst College in 1895
- **Occupation:** Lawyer
- **Political Party:** Republican
- **Vice-President:** Charles G. Dawes
- **Married:** October 4, 1905, to Grace Goodhue
- **Children:** John and Calvin
- **Died:** January 5, 1933

Calvin Coolidge seldom smiled, and he wasted few words. But people liked him for his clear thinking and his dry sense of humor. Once, at a party, a woman told Coolidge that she had bet that she could get him to say more than three words. Silent Cal, as he was known, said, "You lose."

In 1919, as governor of Massachusetts, Coolidge took a firm stand against a strike by Boston policemen. The reputation he gained for supporting law and order helped him win the vice presidency.

After Coolidge replaced Warren G. Harding as president, he forced the resignation of officials who had been involved in the scandals and corruption of Harding's administration. Coolidge easily won the election of 1924. But the victory was offset by a personal loss: the death of his son Calvin, age 16, from blood poisoning.

Coolidge's great goal as president was to promote peace. He supported an international treaty that outlawed war—the Kellogg Pact—and the creation of a World Court to settle international disputes. However, the United States did not join the court, because the Senate did not approve the plan. Coolidge was popular enough to have won a second full term, but he chose not to run.

THE FIRST LADY

Grace Goodhue Coolidge was as relaxed and outgoing as her husband was formal and reserved. She was fond of outdoor sports and animals, and she kept two white collies that became known around the country. Her good taste and sense of fun made her one of the most popular First Ladies.

THE VICE-PRESIDENT

Charles G. Dawes of Ohio had a long career in government administration and diplomacy. After World War I ended, he arranged schedules and loans to help Germany to pay reparations (payments for damages) to the Allies. He shared the 1925 Nobel Peace Prize for his role in this plan, which was called the Dawes Plan.

IN COOLIDGE'S DAY

1924: Congress passed a law making Native Americans U.S. citizens.

1925: John Scopes, a Tennessee teacher, was convicted of violating a state law by teaching Charles Darwin's theory of evolution.

1927: Charles Lindbergh flew solo nonstop across the Atlantic Ocean, the first person to do so. *The Jazz Singer*, the first "talking" movie, was produced.

HERBERT HOOVER

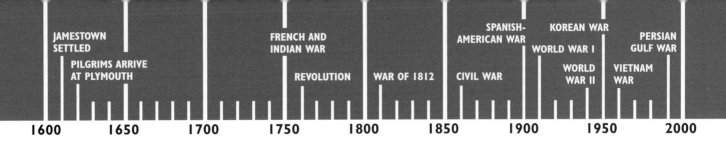

JAMESTOWN SETTLED		FRENCH AND INDIAN WAR			SPANISH-AMERICAN WAR	KOREAN WAR		PERSIAN GULF WAR
PILGRIMS ARRIVE AT PLYMOUTH		REVOLUTION	WAR OF 1812	CIVIL WAR	WORLD WAR I	WORLD WAR II	VIETNAM WAR	
1600	1650	1700	1750	1800	1850	1900	1950	2000

- **Born:** August 10, 1874, in West Branch, Iowa
- **Education:** Graduated from Stanford University in 1895
- **Occupation:** Engineer
- **Political Party:** Republican
- **Vice-President:** Charles Curtis
- **Married:** February 10, 1899, to Lou Henry
- **Children:** Herbert and Allan
- **Died:** October 20, 1965

When Herbert Clark Hoover took office, the United States seemed to be facing a bright, prosperous future. But on October 29, 1929, the stock market crashed. Thousands of investors lost their money. And the crash was just the start of a major economic slump. Businesses failed, and people lost their jobs. By the time Hoover left office, more than 12 million people were out of work, due to what became known as the Great Depression.

Hoover had been a successful mining engineer before entering politics. After World War I, he had directed Allied relief efforts in Europe. As president, he thought at first that the Depression would be short. Rather than aiding unemployed workers, he tried to help the economy by lending money to businesses and local governments. The hope was that they would then hire more workers. But instead, the Depression deepened.

Many people lost their homes and moved into shacks and tents. The large groups of shacks that sprang up around the country became known as Hoovervilles. People criticized the government, and especially the president, for not doing more to help. In the election of 1932, Hoover was soundly defeated by Franklin D. Roosevelt, the Democratic candidate.

THE FIRST LADY

Lou Henry Hoover supported women's rights and worked with groups such as the League of Women Voters. In the White House, she restored several rooms with furniture from the Lincoln and Monroe eras. Three secretaries helped handle her busy schedule.

THE VICE-PRESIDENT

Charles Curtis of Kansas, Herbert Hoover's vice-president, had been a congressman and a senator. As Republican leader in the Senate, he was known for getting the legislators to complete their work on time.

IN HOOVER'S DAY

1930: The U.S. population totaled more than 123 million.

1931: The Empire State Building opened in New York City. Chicago gangster Al Capone, who grew rich through liquor smuggling and other crimes, was convicted of tax evasion.

1932: The so-called Bonus Army—about 15,000 unemployed war veterans—marched on Washington, D.C., to demand payment of a bonus owned by the government.

On the campaign trail.

FRANKLIN D. ROOSEVELT

THE 32ND PRESIDENT (1933-1945)

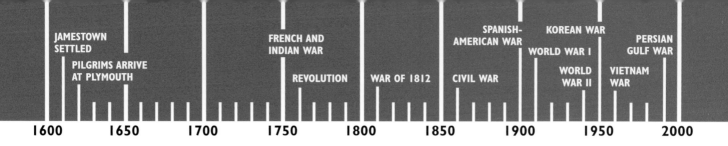

| JAMESTOWN SETTLED | | FRENCH AND INDIAN WAR | | | | SPANISH-AMERICAN WAR | KOREAN WAR | PERSIAN GULF WAR |
| PILGRIMS ARRIVE AT PLYMOUTH | | REVOLUTION | WAR OF 1812 | CIVIL WAR | | WORLD WAR I | WORLD WAR II | VIETNAM WAR |

| 1600 | 1650 | 1700 | 1750 | 1800 | 1850 | 1900 | 1950 | 2000 |

- **Born:** January 30, 1882, in Hyde Park, New York
- **Education:** Graduated from Harvard College in 1903
- **Occupation:** Lawyer
- **Political Party:** Democratic
- **Vice-Presidents:** John Garner, Henry Wallace, and Harry S. Truman
- **Married:** March 17, 1905, to Eleanor Roosevelt
- **Children:** Anna, James, Elliot, Franklin, and John; another son died in infancy
- **Died:** April 12, 1945

Franklin Delano Roosevelt served 12 years as president, longer than any other person. He was elected four times, and he led the country through most of the Depression and World War II. Paralyzed by polio at age 39, he never let his disability dampen his self-confidence or keep him from leadership.

FDR, as he was called, belonged to a large and wealthy New York family. He was brought up to believe that the rich had a duty to serve society. He admired Theodore Roosevelt, a member of a branch of his family, and tried to follow in his footsteps. Like TR, Franklin Roosevelt was an assistant secretary of the navy. He was the Democratic candidate for vice-president in 1920. But the Democrats lost, and the next year, FDR was stricken with polio.

Many people thought that his political career was over. But Franklin Roosevelt fought back. He learned to get around with a wheelchair or crutches. He exercised in swimming pools and in the mineral waters at Warm Springs, Georgia. And he kept up his political contacts. In 1928, he surprised everyone by winning election as governor of New York. When the Great Depression began, he took the lead in setting up programs to help the jobless. Soon his name was known around the country. Promising Americans a

"new deal," Roosevelt won the 1932 presidential election easily.

FDR's first two terms were taken up largely with fighting the Depression. But by the mid-1930s, trouble was brewing abroad. Fascist governments in Germany, Italy, and Japan were threatening war. World War II broke out in Europe in 1939, when Germany overran Poland. At first, the United States sent supplies to Britain and other Allies in the fight against Germany, but it stayed out of the fighting. Then, on December 7, 1941, Japan attacked U.S. Navy ships at Pearl Harbor, Hawaii. Calling this "a date which will live in infamy," President Roosevelt asked Congress to declare war.

FDR addresses the nation in 1941.

Soon American troops were fighting on two fronts—in Europe and in the Pacific. Roosevelt helped hold the Allies together. And he helped keep Americans behind the war effort, rallying them with weekly radio talks—"fireside chats." By early in 1945, the war had turned in the Allies' favor. The Allies were closing on Berlin, the German capital, and gaining in the Pacific, too. But Roosevelt did not live to see the end of the war. Just a few months after the start of his fourth term, he died suddenly of a stroke while at Warm Springs.

FDR'S NEW DEAL

When Franklin Delano Roosevelt took office in 1933, the country was at the darkest time of the Depression. All over the country, banks and businesses were failing. Millions of people were losing their jobs and their savings. Roosevelt knew that the first step in rebuilding the economy was to make people confident about the future. "The only thing we have to fear is fear itself," he said in his inauguration speech.

To stop panicky depositors from withdrawing their money, Roosevelt declared a nationwide "bank holiday." With the banks closed, he called a special session of Congress and began to put in place the programs that become known as the New Deal. Some of these programs provided loans and jobs, mainly in public-works projects. Other programs guaranteed people's bank deposits and regulated the stock market. Later New Deal reforms included old-age pensions for workers and support payments to the disabled. This sort of social involvement was new ground for the federal government, and some people were alarmed by it. But for the most part, FDR's New Deal was welcomed. It helped millions of people get back to work.

Hungry men join a Washington, D. C., soup-kitchen line during the Great Depression.

A TWO-TERM LIMIT

In 1940, when Franklin D. Roosevelt ran for a third term as president, many people were shocked. In the 150 years since George Washington had declined to seek a third term, no president had served more than two. The Republican candidate in 1940, Wendel Wilkie, based his campaign on this fact. But that year, and again in 1944, American voters decided that they needed Roosevelt's experience to handle the nation's problems. After Roosevelt's death, however, there was concern that one person had been able to hold the nation's highest office so long. As a result, the 22nd Amendment to the Constitution, which was approved in 1951, limited future presidents to two terms in office.

This political cartoon expresses confidence that FDR will serve a third term as president.

THE FIRST LADY

Eleanor Roosevelt was one of the most active and most beloved First Ladies in history. She had her own radio program and a newspaper column, held weekly news conferences, and traveled around the country. After FDR's death, she became a delegate to the United Nations. She was especially known for her work on behalf of minorities, women, and the poor. Eleanor was a distant cousin of Franklin and a niece of Teddy Roosevelt.

Garner   Wallace   Truman

THE VICE-PRESIDENTS

John Garner of Texas was vice-president during Franklin Roosevelt's first two terms. He had been speaker of the House of Representatives. Henry Wallace, who had been secretary of agriculture, was vice-president for Roosevelt's third term. And Harry S. Truman, a senator from Missouri, was elected for Roosevelt's fourth term.

IN ROOSEVELT'S DAY

1933: The 21st Amendment ended Prohibition.
1937: The German dirigible *Hindenburg* exploded on landing in New Jersey, killing 35 people.
1940: The U.S. population was 132 million.
1942: The first nuclear chain reaction was created.

HARRY S. TRUMAN

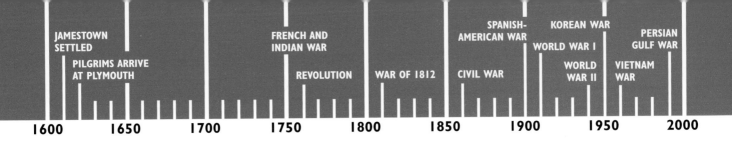

JAMESTOWN SETTLED		FRENCH AND INDIAN WAR			SPANISH-AMERICAN WAR	KOREAN WAR	PERSIAN GULF WAR	
PILGRIMS ARRIVE AT PLYMOUTH		REVOLUTION	WAR OF 1812	CIVIL WAR	WORLD WAR I	WORLD WAR II	VIETNAM WAR	

1600   1650   1700   1750   1800   1850   1900   1950   2000

- **Born:** May 8, 1884, in Lamar, Missouri
- **Education:** Attended University of Kansas City Law School (1923-1925)
- **Occupation:** Farmer; businessman
- **Political Party:** Democratic
- **Vice-President:** Alben W. Barkley
- **Married:** June 28, 1919, to Elizabeth Wallace
- **Children:** Mary Margaret ("Margaret")
- **Died:** December 26, 1972

On April 12, 1945, less than three months after he had become vice-president, Harry S. Truman was suddenly called to the White House. President Franklin D. Roosevelt had died. Truman was sworn in as president that day.

A plain-spoken man known for his honesty, Truman faced enormous challenges as president. World War II was still raging. Germany surrendered a month later, but the war with Japan dragged on. Truman made a hard choice. He decided to drop two atomic bombs on Japan, the first time such weapons were used. He hoped that these terrible weapons would shorten the war. They did—peace talks began August 10, 1945, four days after the first bomb fell.

Truman's domestic policies, though, did not meet with much success, and he had trouble dealing with Congress. Republicans were certain that their candidate, Thomas Dewey, would win the 1948 presidential election. Truman surprised everyone with his upset victory.

The programs and policies of Truman's administration helped shape the postwar world. The Marshall Plan aided war-torn countries. The Truman Doctrine announced U.S. opposition to communism. When Communist North Korea invaded South Korea in 1950, Truman sent U.S. troops to defend South Korea. Truman supported U.S. entry into the United Nations.

THE FIRST LADY

Elizabeth ("Bess") Wallace Truman had been Harry Truman's childhood sweetheart. He often referred to her jokingly as "the boss," and to their daughter Margaret as "the boss's boss." The First Lady had little taste for the formalities of White House life. During Truman's second term, the White House needed extensive repairs. The First Family moved out and kept entertaining to a minimum.

THE VICE-PRESIDENT

Alben W. Barkley had been a senator from Kentucky for more than 20 years when he was picked as Truman's running mate in 1948. (Truman had no vice-president while serving out Roosevelt's term in office.) He played an active part in the Truman administration. Then he returned to the Senate, serving from 1954 until his death in 1956.

IN TRUMAN'S DAY

1945: The United Nations charter was signed by delegates from 50 countries meeting in San Francisco, California.

1947: Jackie Robinson joined the Brooklyn Dodgers, becoming the first black player in major league baseball.

1948: The United States and ten other countries formed the North Atlantic Treaty Organization (NATO) for the defense of Western Europe.

1950: The U.S. population was 151 million.

DWIGHT D. EISENHOWER

THE 34TH PRESIDENT (1953-1961)

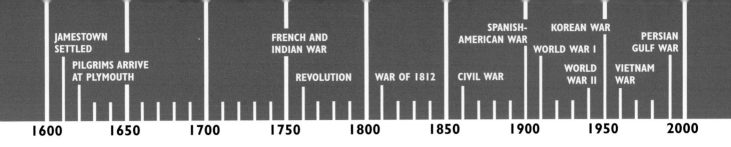

JAMESTOWN SETTLED		FRENCH AND INDIAN WAR		SPANISH-AMERICAN WAR	KOREAN WAR	PERSIAN GULF WAR
PILGRIMS ARRIVE AT PLYMOUTH		REVOLUTION	WAR OF 1812	CIVIL WAR	WORLD WAR I / WORLD WAR II	VIETNAM WAR

1600   1650   1700   1750   1800   1850   1900   1950   2000

- **Born:** October 14, 1890, in Denison, Texas
- **Education:** Graduated from the U.S. Military Academy at West Point in 1915
- **Occupation:** Soldier
- **Political Party:** Republican
- **Vice-President:** Richard M. Nixon
- **Married:** July 1, 1916, to Mamie Doud
- **Children:** David and John
- **Died:** March 25, 1969

When Dwight David Eisenhower ran for president in 1952, he was already one of the most famous men in the country. A five-star army general—the highest rank—he had led Allied forces to victory in Europe in World War II. Then General Eisenhower had commanded North Atlantic Treaty Organization (NATO) forces.

Ike, as he was often called, was a career soldier who had never been very active in politics. But he decided to run for president as a Republican because he felt that party best represented the rights of individuals. "I Like Ike" was an appropriate campaign slogan for Eisenhower. With his wide grin, easy manners, and generous, open nature, it was hard not to like him.

Eisenhower ended the Korean War—which was a campaign promise—soon after he took office. His two terms were mostly a time of peace and prosperity for the nation.

But Cold War tensions grew between the United States and the Soviet Union. One of the worst moments came in 1960, when an American U-2 spy plane was shot down over the Soviet Union. And at home, the civil rights movement was gathering steam. In 1957, Eisenhower sent troops to enforce a court order ending school segregation in Little Rock, Arkansas.

THE FIRST LADY

Mamie Doud Eisenhower estimated that during her husband's army career, she moved their household 27 times. In fact, the Eisenhowers lived in the White House longer—eight years—than anywhere else up to that time. Mamie was a popular First Lady who set fashion trends with her short bangs and fondness for pink.

THE VICE-PRESIDENT

Richard M. Nixon was a senator from California when he was picked as Eisenhower's running mate. He had gained fame for his strong anti-Communist views.

IN EISENHOWER'S DAY

1954: Jonas Salk developed a polio vaccine. The Supreme Court ruled that racially segregated schools were in violation of the Constitution.

1955: Martin Luther King, Jr., led a boycott of segregated buses in Montgomery, Alabama.

1956: Rock singer Elvis Presley's first television appearance was watched by a record-high audience of 54 million people.

1958: The United States launched its first satellite, *Explorer 1*.

1959: Alaska and Hawaii became states.

1960: The U.S. population was 179 million.

JOHN F. KENNEDY

THE 35TH PRESIDENT (1961-1963)

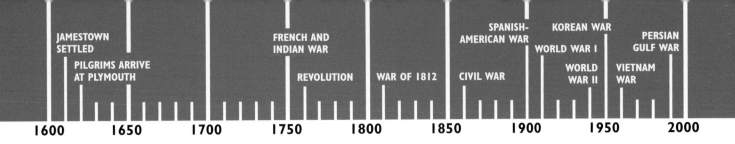

					SPANISH-	KOREAN WAR	
JAMESTOWN SETTLED			FRENCH AND INDIAN WAR		AMERICAN WAR	WORLD WAR I	PERSIAN GULF WAR
	PILGRIMS ARRIVE AT PLYMOUTH			REVOLUTION	WAR OF 1812	CIVIL WAR	WORLD WAR II	VIETNAM WAR

1600   1650   1700   1750   1800   1850   1900   1950   2000

- **Born:** May 29, 1917, in Brookline, Massachusetts
- **Education:** Graduated from Harvard University in 1940
- **Occupation:** Businessman
- **Political Party:** Democratic
- **Vice-President:** Lyndon B. Johnson
- **Married:** September 12, 1953, to Jacqueline Bouvier
- **Children:** Caroline and John; another son died in infancy
- **Died:** November 22, 1963

John Fitzgerald Kennedy ("JFK") had served less than three years as president when he was assassinated. But in that short time, he captured the imagination of the country with his youth, energy, and charm. Because of him, Americans dreamed of going to the moon and volunteered to join the Peace Corps to help people in other countries. Kennedy promised to "get the country moving," and he did.

Jack Kennedy, as he was known, grew up in a large, wealthy Boston family. He attended top schools and served in the navy during World War II, as commander of a PT (torpedo) boat in the Pacific Ocean. When the boat was attacked by the Japanese, he took heroic actions to save his men. He won several medals. But he also injured his back, which troubled him for the rest of his life.

Kennedy was just 28 when he was elected to the House of Representatives in 1946. After six years in the House, he was elected to the Senate. In 1960, he was chosen as the Democratic presidential candidate, to run against Richard Nixon, the then vice-president. The campaign included the first televised presidential debates. Kennedy won the election by a narrow margin. At age 43, he was the youngest person ever elected president of the United States.

In his inaugural speech, John Kennedy urged Americans to "ask not what your country can do for you; ask what you can do for your country." He did not serve long enough to reach many of his goals, including stronger civil rights laws. But he began several programs that had long-lasting effects. One was the Peace Corps, which sends volunteers to help people in developing countries. Kennedy also set a major goal for America's space program: a manned flight to the moon.

Cold War tensions were high in the Kennedy years. In East Germany, Communist authorities built the Berlin Wall to divide Communist East Berlin from non-Communist West Berlin. Kennedy visited West Berlin to show American support, and he was greeted with wild cheers. On the other side of the world, in South Vietnam, a bloody civil war erupted between Communists and non-Communists. Kennedy sent U.S. military advisers to South Vietnam, the first step in American involvement there.

JFK with Soviet Premier Nikita Khrushchev.

On November 22, 1963, Kennedy was in Dallas, Texas, to make a speech. As his motorcade passed cheering crowds, he was fatally shot. His death shocked and saddened people around the world. One foreign leader summed up their feelings. He said that with John F. Kennedy's death, "a flame went out for all those who had hoped for a just peace and a better life."

Halloween at the Kennedy White House.

THE KENNEDY WHITE HOUSE

During John F. Kennedy's term, the White House became a center of art and culture. The president and First Lady invited top performers and musicians, and they entertained elegantly. Jacqueline Kennedy worked with designers to decorate the mansion with historically accurate furnishings. Meanwhile, the two young Kennedy children helped keep the White House lively.

Carolyn was just three and John, Jr., just two months old when they moved in. Before long, there were swings and a tree house on the grounds—not to mention Caroline's pony, Macaroni. As John, Jr., grew older, he turned his father's desk into a fort. The Kennedys tried to keep the children's lives private. But it was impossible—newspaper readers loved stories about the kids.

KENNEDY AND CUBA

Two of the most serious crises of John Kennedy's term involved Cuba. This Caribbean country lies only about 100 miles off the southern tip of Florida. In

A quarter-million people hear JFK speak in West Berlin, in West Germany.

1959, a revolution there brought Fidel Castro to power. Castro allied his country with the Soviet Union, and that worried the United States. In April 1961, Kennedy backed a group of Cuban exiles who tried to overthrow Castro. Their invasion, at the Bay of Pigs, failed. It was a great embarrassment for the United States.

Eighteen months later, Kennedy learned that the Soviet Union was placing missiles in Cuba, where they could easily strike the United States. He demanded that the Soviets withdraw the weapons. He also ordered the navy to stop all ships headed for Cuba. For a week, the world held its breath, fearing that the crisis would lead to war. But the Soviets finally backed down, and the missiles were withdrawn.

ASSASSINATION THEORIES

Within hours of John Kennedy's shooting, police arrested a suspect. He was Lee Harvey Oswald, a former Marine who had once lived in the Soviet Union. But Oswald was never tried for the crime. Two days later, while he was in police custody, he was shot by Jack Ruby, a Dallas, Texas nightclub owner.

Ever since, Kennedy's assassination has been surrounded by questions. Strong evidence linked Oswald to the crime. But what were his motives? Did he act alone? A government panel, the Warren Commission, was appointed to investigate. It decided that Oswald was the assassin and that he acted alone. Still, some people believe that a second gunman also shot at the president. Many think that there was a conspiracy—by organized crime, foreign agents, or even government officials—to kill the president. The evidence for these theories is weak. But they still continue to fascinate people.

THE FIRST LADY

Jacqueline ("Jackie") Bouvier Kennedy was known for her grace and style. As First Lady, she was constantly in the public eye, but she found politics boring and cherished her privacy. Her poise when her husband was assassinated was widely admired. When she died in 1994, Jackie was buried next to JFK in Arlington National Cemetary in Virginia.

THE VICE-PRESIDENT

Lyndon B. Johnson, a powerful senator from Texas, was edged out by John Kennedy for the 1960 Democratic nomination. Kennedy then chose Johnson as his running mate. When Kennedy was shot, Johnson was riding in the same motorcade, two cars back. He was sworn in as president that day aboard *Air Force One*, the presidential plane, on the way back to Washington, D.C.

IN KENNEDY'S DAY

1961: Alan Shepherd, Jr., became the first American in space.

1962: Rachel Carson's book *Silent Spring* drew attention to the dangers of pesticides.

1963: The United States, Britain, and the Soviet Union signed a treaty limiting tests of nuclear weapons. Civil rights leader Martin Luther King, Jr., delivered a moving speech—"I Have a Dream"—at a huge rally in Washington, D.C.

LYNDON B. JOHNSON

THE 36TH PRESIDENT (1963-1969)

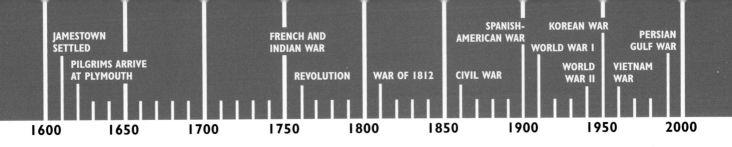

				SPANISH-AMERICAN WAR	KOREAN WAR	
JAMESTOWN SETTLED		FRENCH AND INDIAN WAR			WORLD WAR I	PERSIAN GULF WAR
PILGRIMS ARRIVE AT PLYMOUTH		REVOLUTION	WAR OF 1812	CIVIL WAR	WORLD WAR II	VIETNAM WAR

| 1600 | 1650 | 1700 | 1750 | 1800 | 1850 | 1900 | 1950 | 2000 |

- **Born:** August 27, 1908, near Stonewall, Texas
- **Education:** Graduated from Southwest Texas State Teachers College in 1930
- **Occupation:** Teacher
- **Political Party:** Democratic
- **Vice-President:** Hubert Humphrey
- **Married:** November 17, 1934, to Claudia Taylor
- **Children:** Lynda Bird and Luci
- **Died:** January 22, 1973

Lyndon Baines Johnson grew up in poverty in rural Texas. Over the years, he worked his way up to become an important senator, and then vice-president. But he never forgot his roots. When John F. Kennedy was assassinated and Johnson succeeded (followed) him as president, he did much to improve life for the poor.

Soon after he was sworn in, Johnson outlined a group of social programs that he called the Great Society. The programs included medical insurance for the poor and elderly (Medicaid and Medicare) and preschool education for poor children (Head Start). The president also backed the Civil Rights Act of 1964, a strong law that barred discrimination in employment and other areas.

Johnson's experience in the Senate helped him build support for his programs in Congress. He was easily elected president in 1964. But meanwhile, he took steps that got the United States deeply involved in a very unpopular war. South Vietnam, a U.S. ally, was fighting Communist rebels and troops from North Vietnam. By 1968, thousands of U.S. soldiers were fighting there, too. The Vietnam War deeply divided Americans. Many who opposed it blamed Johnson. He decided not to seek another term.

THE FIRST LADY

Claudia Taylor Johnson was nicknamed "Lady Bird" as a young child, and that was how she was known throughout her life. As First Lady, she directed a highway beautification program that limited the number of billboards and improved plantings along roadways.

THE VICE-PRESIDENT

Hubert Humphrey, who had been a senator from Minnesota, chaired several government councils as Lyndon Johnson's vice-president. When Johnson decided not to run for reelection in 1968, Humphrey was chosen as the Democratic candidate. He lost the election but later returned to the Senate.

IN JOHNSON'S DAY

1964: The Beatles, a four-member British rock group, made a wildly successful U.S. tour.

1967: Thurgood Marshall became the first African American to serve on the U.S. Supreme Court.

1968: Civil rights leader Martin Luther King, Jr., was assassinated in April. Senator Robert F. Kennedy, a brother of John F. Kennedy, was assassinated in June.

Johnson greets U. S. troops in Vietnam.

95

RICHARD M. NIXON

THE 37TH PRESIDENT (1969-1974)

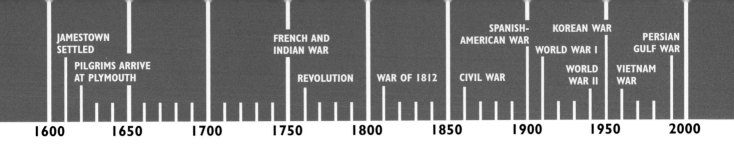

	JAMESTOWN SETTLED			FRENCH AND INDIAN WAR				SPANISH-AMERICAN WAR	KOREAN WAR	
	PILGRIMS ARRIVE AT PLYMOUTH				REVOLUTION	WAR OF 1812		CIVIL WAR	WORLD WAR I	PERSIAN GULF WAR

1600   1650   1700   1750   1800   1850   1900   1950   2000

- **Born:** January 9, 1913, in Yorba Linda, California
- **Education:** Graduated from Whittier College in 1934 and Duke University Law School in 1937
- **Occupation:** Lawyer
- **Political Party:** Republican
- **Vice-Presidents:** Spiro T. Agnew and Gerald R. Ford
- **Married:** June 21, 1940, to Thelma Ryan
- **Children:** Patricia and Julie
- **Died:** April 22, 1994

Richard Milhous Nixon was the first person to resign the American presidency. He was forced to step down as a result of the scandal known as the Watergate affair. Although he did much as president, the scandal overshadowed his accomplishments.

Nixon was elected in 1968 partly on his promise to end the Vietnam War. He did, although not until U.S. troops had fought for three more years. Some of Nixon's greatest achievements were in relations with other countries. He signed an arms control agreement with the Soviet Union. And in 1972 he visited China, ending 25 years of icy relations with that country. These steps helped to ease the tensions of the Cold War.

The Watergate scandal began during the 1972 presidential campaign. Workers for a committee to reelect Nixon were caught breaking into Democratic party headquarters at the Watergate apartment complex in Washington, D.C. Nixon and his aides tried to cover up their connection to the burglary. Nixon won the election. But in the end his role in the cover-up, as well as other campaign irregularities, was discovered. He finally resigned to avoid almost certain impeachment.

THE FIRST LADY

Christened Thelma Catherine Ryan, the First Lady was called Pat all her life because she was born on St. Patrick's Day. She was a tireless supporter of her husband throughout his long political career.

THE VICE-PRESIDENTS

Spiro T. Agnew was the governor of Maryland when he was elected vice-president in 1968. He won reelection with Richard Nixon in 1972 but resigned in 1973, when it was found that he had taken bribes and avoided paying his income taxes.

Gerald R. Ford, a well-respected Michigan congressman, was chosen by Nixon to replace Agnew. His appointment followed procedures set out in the 25th Amendment to the Constitution.

IN NIXON'S DAY

1969: Astronaut Neil Armstrong became the first person to set foot on the moon. Some 400,000 young people flocked to the Woodstock music festival, in upstate New York.

1970: Four students were killed by the National Guard during an antiwar protest at Kent State University in Ohio. The first Earth Day was held to increase awareness of the environment. The U.S. population reached 203 million.

1971: The 26th Amendment lowered the voting age to 18.

GERALD R. FORD

THE 38TH PRESIDENT (1974-1977)

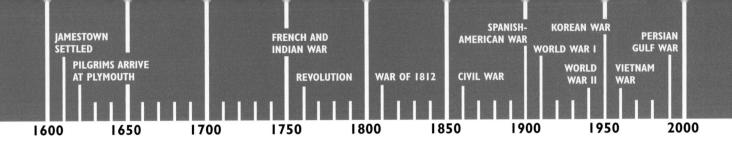

| | | | | FRENCH AND INDIAN WAR | | | SPANISH-AMERICAN WAR | KOREAN WAR | PERSIAN GULF WAR |

JAMESTOWN SETTLED

PILGRIMS ARRIVE AT PLYMOUTH

FRENCH AND INDIAN WAR

REVOLUTION

WAR OF 1812

CIVIL WAR

SPANISH-AMERICAN WAR

WORLD WAR I

WORLD WAR II

KOREAN WAR

VIETNAM WAR

PERSIAN GULF WAR

1600   1650   1700   1750   1800   1850   1900   1950   2000

- **Born:** July 14, 1913, in Omaha, Nebraska
- **Education:** Graduated from the University of Michigan in 1935 and from Yale University in 1941
- **Occupation:** Lawyer
- **Political Party:** Republican
- **Vice-President:** Nelson A. Rockefeller
- **Married:** October 15, 1948, to Elizabeth Bloomer
- **Children:** Michael, John, Steven, and Susan

Gerald Rudolph Ford was the first person to step into the presidency without being elected as either the president or vice-president. He was appointed vice-president in 1973, after Spiro Agnew resigned that post in a bribery scandal. And he became president when Richard Nixon resigned over the Watergate scandal. After so much turmoil in the White House, Ford's honesty and openness did much to restore faith in the presidency.

Jerry Ford, as he was called, had been a college football star and coach before he entered law and politics. He served for 25 years as a Michigan congressman, finally becoming the leader of the Republicans in the House of Representatives. During his years in Congress, Ford earned a solid reputation for honesty and fairness.

After he was sworn in as president, Gerald Ford pardoned Nixon for any wrongs he might have done as president. This angered Americans who felt that Nixon should have been tried in the legal system. But Ford wanted the country to move on and put the Watergate affair behind it. Ford also faced economic problems and other difficulties left over from the Nixon years. He was personally popular, but he was not viewed as a strong national leader. He lost the 1976 election to James ("Jimmy") E. Carter.

THE FIRST LADY

Elizabeth ("Betty") Bloomer Ford was admired for her honesty and courage. She underwent surgery for breast cancer soon after her husband took office, but she quickly recovered and took on the duties of White House hostess. Betty especially enjoyed dances (she had danced professionally before her marriage). She was a strong supporter of equal rights for women.

THE VICE-PRESIDENT

Nelson A. Rockefeller was appointed vice-president when Gerald Ford became president. A member of one of the country's best-known wealthy families, Rockefeller had served as the governor of New York. He long held hopes of becoming president but never acheived this goal.

IN FORD'S DAY

1975: Saigon, the capital of South Vietnam, fell to North Vietnam. The United States helped evacuate South Vietnamese refugees. Cambodia seized the U.S.S. *Mayaguez,* and President Ford ordered a rescue mission. The president survives two separate assassination attempts.

1976: *Viking I* and *Viking 2,* unmanned U.S. spacecraft, landed on Mars. The United States celebrated the bicentennial (the 200th anniversary) of its founding.

JAMES E. CARTER

THE 39TH PRESIDENT (1977-1981)

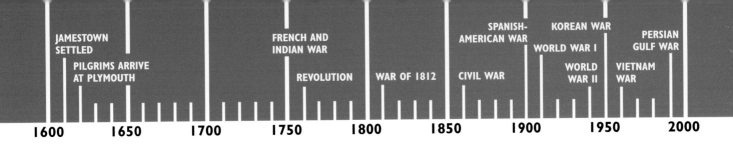

JAMESTOWN SETTLED

PILGRIMS ARRIVE AT PLYMOUTH

FRENCH AND INDIAN WAR

REVOLUTION

WAR OF 1812

CIVIL WAR

SPANISH-AMERICAN WAR

KOREAN WAR

WORLD WAR I

WORLD WAR II

VIETNAM WAR

PERSIAN GULF WAR

1600   1650   1700   1750   1800   1850   1900   1950   2000

- **Born:** October 1, 1924, in Plains, Georgia
- **Education:** Graduated from the U.S. Naval Academy in 1946
- **Occupation:** Farmer
- **Political Party:** Democratic
- **Vice-President:** Walter F. Mondale
- **Married:** July 7, 1946, to Rosalynn Smith
- **Children:** John, James, Jeffrey, and Amy

When James Earl Carter, Jr.— known as "Jimmy" Carter—decided to run for president, few people outside his home state, Georgia, knew his name. But after the scandals of the Nixon years, many Americans were ready for a change. They hoped that someone new—someone who had not been in national government—would get the country moving forward.

Carter had been a navy officer and a successful peanut farmer before he entered state politics, rising quickly to governor of Georgia. He was widely known for his honesty and decency. As president, Carter discarded some of the frills and formality of the office. He sold the presidential yacht and often dressed casually.

One of Jimmy Carter's great achievements was negotiating a peace treaty, the Camp David Accords, between Israel and Egypt. It ended 30 years of hatred between those countries. Carter made human rights the focus of his foreign policy. At home, he set up programs to help the country save energy supplies. But he faced serious problems. Congress defeated many of his proposals for reform. Unemployment was high, and so was inflation—that is, prices were rising quickly. And in the Middle East, radicals took over the U.S. embassy in Teheran, Iran, and held Americans there hostage.

Many voters thought that the president should have done more to solve these problems. He was not elected to a second term.

THE FIRST LADY

Rosalynn Smith Carter played an important part in her husband's administration. She often sat in on cabinet meetings and high-level briefings. She also traveled abroad to represent the government.

THE VICE-PRESIDENT

Walter F. Mondale of Minnesota had served in the Senate before becoming Jimmy Carter's vice-president. He was active in that role, visiting Congress to speak for Carter's programs and making many diplomatic visits around the world. Mondale ran for president in 1984, but he was defeated by Ronald Reagan.

IN CARTER'S DAY

1978: The United States agreed to give Panama full control of the Panama Canal by the year 2000.

1979: A major accident occurred at the Three Mile Island nuclear power plant near Harrisburg, Pennsylvania.

1980: The U.S. population was more than 226 million. Mount St. Helens, a volcano in Washington State, erupted. Sixty people were killed.

RONALD REAGAN

THE 40TH PRESIDENT (1981-1989)

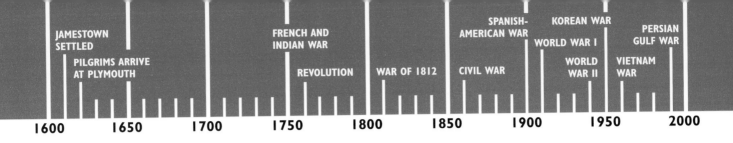

JAMESTOWN SETTLED

PILGRIMS ARRIVE AT PLYMOUTH

FRENCH AND INDIAN WAR

REVOLUTION

WAR OF 1812

CIVIL WAR

SPANISH-AMERICAN WAR

KOREAN WAR

WORLD WAR I

WORLD WAR II

VIETNAM WAR

PERSIAN GULF WAR

1600 1650 1700 1750 1800 1850 1900 1950 2000

- **Born:** February 6, 1911, in Tampico, Illinois
- **Education:** Graduated from Eureka College in 1932
- **Occupation:** Actor
- **Political Party:** Republican
- **Vice-President:** George Bush
- **Married:** January 24, 1940, to Jane Wyman; March 4, 1952, to Nancy Davis
- **Children:** Maureen, Michael, Patricia, and Ronald, Jr.

Many people did not take Ronald Wilson Reagan seriously when he first entered politics in the 1960s. Reagan had been a radio announcer and a successful movie actor. He was past 50 when he made his last film and switched to politics. But he rose quickly as a spokesman for conservative Republicans. He served two terms as governor of California. Then, in 1980, he captured the Republican presidential nomination and won the election.

As president, Reagan set out to build up the U.S. military while cutting government spending and taxes. He took a strong stand against communism and backed anti-Communist fighters in Central America and Afghanistan. In 1983, he sent U.S. troops to Grenada, a Caribbean island, after radicals took power there. But relations with the Soviet Union improved.

Not all of Reagan's policies succeeded. Despite budget cuts, government spending rose. By the end of Reagan's two terms, the United States was deeply in debt. And Reagan's administration was marked by controversy: White House officials had secret dealings with Iran, and they sent money to rebels in Nicaragua against the wishes of Congress. Even with these troubles, however, Reagan himself remained popular. Some critics even referred to him as "the Teflon President," meaning that bad news did not "stick" to him.

THE FIRST LADY

Nancy Davis Reagan married Ronald Reagan three years after his first marriage, to actress Jane Wyman, ended in divorce. Nancy was also an actress. As First Lady, she favored formal, elegant entertaining.

THE VICE-PRESIDENT

George Bush had had a long career as a public official before becoming Reagan's vice-president. He made a bid for the 1980 Republican presidential nomination. But when Reagan won it, Bush accepted the vice-presidential slot and supported his former rival.

IN REAGAN'S DAY

1981: Iran released the 52 Americans whom it had held hostage for 444 days. Sandra Day O'Connor became the first woman on the U.S. Supreme Court.

1985: "Live Aid," a 17-hour televised rock concert, raised $470 million for victims of famine in Africa.

1986: Martin Luther King Day was observed as a federal holiday for the first time. The space shuttle *Challenger* exploded on takeoff, killing all seven people aboard.

Soviet leader Mikhail Gorbachev with President Reagan and Vice-President Bush.

GEORGE BUSH

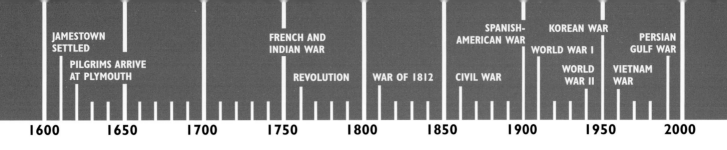

| 1600 | 1650 | 1700 | 1750 | 1800 | 1850 | 1900 | 1950 | 2000 |

JAMESTOWN SETTLED

PILGRIMS ARRIVE AT PLYMOUTH

FRENCH AND INDIAN WAR

REVOLUTION

WAR OF 1812

CIVIL WAR

SPANISH-AMERICAN WAR

KOREAN WAR

WORLD WAR I

WORLD WAR II

VIETNAM WAR

PERSIAN GULF WAR

Born: June 12, 1924, in Milton, Massachusetts

- **Education:** Graduated from Yale University in 1948
- **Occupation:** Businessman
- **Political Party:** Republican
- **Vice-President:** James Danforth Quayle
- **Married:** January 6, 1945, to Barbara Pierce
- **Children:** George, John ("Jeb"), Neil, Marvin, and Dorothy; another daughter died in early childhood

George Herbert Walker Bush took office at an exciting time. Between 1989 and 1991, Communist governments fell throughout Eastern Europe. Finally, the Soviet Union collapsed. The Cold War was finally over. Part of Bush's job as president was to define the U.S. role in this dramatically changing world.

Bush had plenty of experience for the job. He had served in Congress. He had represented the United States in the United Nations and as a diplomat in China. He had directed the Central Intelligence Agency. And he had been vice-president for eight years under Ronald Reagan.

Before becoming a public official, Bush had served as a navy pilot in World War II. A graduate of top East Coast private schools, he had succeeded in the rough-and-tumble Texas oil business.

U.S. troops went into action three times during Bush's presidency: in Panama, in the Persian Gulf region, and in Somalia. The 1991 Persian Gulf War was the largest operation. Troops from the United States and other allied nations liberated Kuwait, which had been invaded by Iraq in 1990. Bush's firm action against Iraq was popular. But by the end of his term, the United States was in a deep economic slump. Bush's popularity dropped, and he lost the 1992 election to William ("Bill") Jefferson Clinton.

THE FIRST LADY

Barbara Pierce Bush once described herself as "everybody's grandmother." Her warmth and wit made her a popular First Lady. She made promoting literacy her special cause during her White House years.

THE VICE-PRESIDENT

James Danforth Quayle, a conservative senator from Indiana, was only 41 when he became Bush's vice-president.

IN BUSH'S DAY

1989: The largest oil spill in U.S. history occured when the *Exxon Valdez* struck a reef in Prince William Sound in Alaska. An earthquake in the San Francisco area of California killed 62 people.

1990: The U.S. population neared 249 million.

1992: U.S. troops went to Somalia, in Africa, to spearhead a famine-relief effort.

President Bush visits U.S. troops in the Persian Gulf region.

WILLIAM J. CLINTON

THE 42ND PRESIDENT (1993-2001)

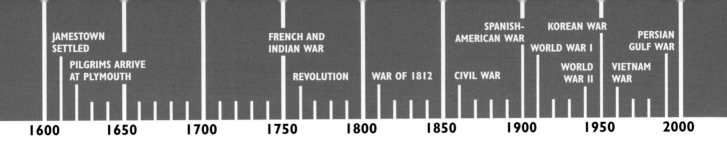

| JAMESTOWN SETTLED | PILGRIMS ARRIVE AT PLYMOUTH | FRENCH AND INDIAN WAR | REVOLUTION | WAR OF 1812 | CIVIL WAR | SPANISH-AMERICAN WAR | WORLD WAR I | KOREAN WAR | WORLD WAR II | VIETNAM WAR | PERSIAN GULF WAR |

| 1600 | 1650 | 1700 | 1750 | 1800 | 1850 | 1900 | 1950 | 2000 |

- **Born:** August 19, 1946, in Hope, Arkansas
- **Education:** Graduated from Georgetown University in 1968 and Yale Law School in 1973
- **Occupation:** Lawyer
- **Political Party:** Democratic
- **Vice-President:** Albert Gore, Jr.
- **Married:** 1975, to Hillary Rodham
- **Children:** Chelsea

A campaign that promised change swept William Jefferson Clinton to the presidency. But Bill Clinton, as he was known, faced challenges in bringing about many of the reforms and changes that he wanted.

Clinton was just 32 years old when he was elected governor of Arkansas, and he went on to serve five terms. He was not well known outside his home state when he began his campaign for the presidency. But Americans were ready for a new face and a new approach to the country's problems. Clinton was the first person of his generation—the generation born after World War II—to be elected president.

Clinton trimmed the federal government's mounting budget deficits and developed a plan to reform America's health care system. But this plan faced steep opposition in Congress, and it did not pass. In 1994, Republicans won control of Congress for the first time in 40 years. After that, Clinton's programs and policies faced even stronger opposition.

Clinton was praised for his handling of a crisis in Haiti. In 1994, U.S. troops had been ready to invade Haiti to return its deposed president to power. Last-minute talks avoided an invasion, and the Haitian president, Bertrand Aristide, returned in a peaceful transition of power.

In 1998, Clinton visited China and urged its leaders to allow more democracy. That same year, Clinton called for increased controls on nuclear weapons after India and Pakistan tested such weapons.

THE FIRST LADY

Hillary Rodham Clinton was a lawyer known especially for her work in the field of children's rights. She led the team that prepared the Clinton health care proposal. She entered the New York State senatorial race in February 2000, and won the Democratic nomination on May 16. On November 7, 2000, Hillary Clinton became the first sitting First Lady to win elective office when she became a U.S. Senator.

THE VICE-PRESIDENT

Albert Gore, Jr., of Tennessee, had served in the House of Representatives and the Senate. He was a respected expert on environmental and arms control issues. He ran for president in the election of 2000, winning the popular vote but losing to George W. Bush by four electoral votes.

IN CLINTON'S DAY

1993: A terrorist bomb exploded in the underground parking garage of the World Trade Center in New York City.

1994: A severe earthquake struck Los Angeles, California.

1995: A terrorist bomb exploded at a federal office building in Oklahoma City, killing 160 people. It was the worst act of terrorism ever in U.S. territory.

1998: House of Representatives voted to impeach Clinton on charges of perjury and obstruction of justice.

1999: Senate acquitted Clinton of impeachment charges.

GEORGE W. BUSH

THE 43RD PRESIDENT (2001-   )

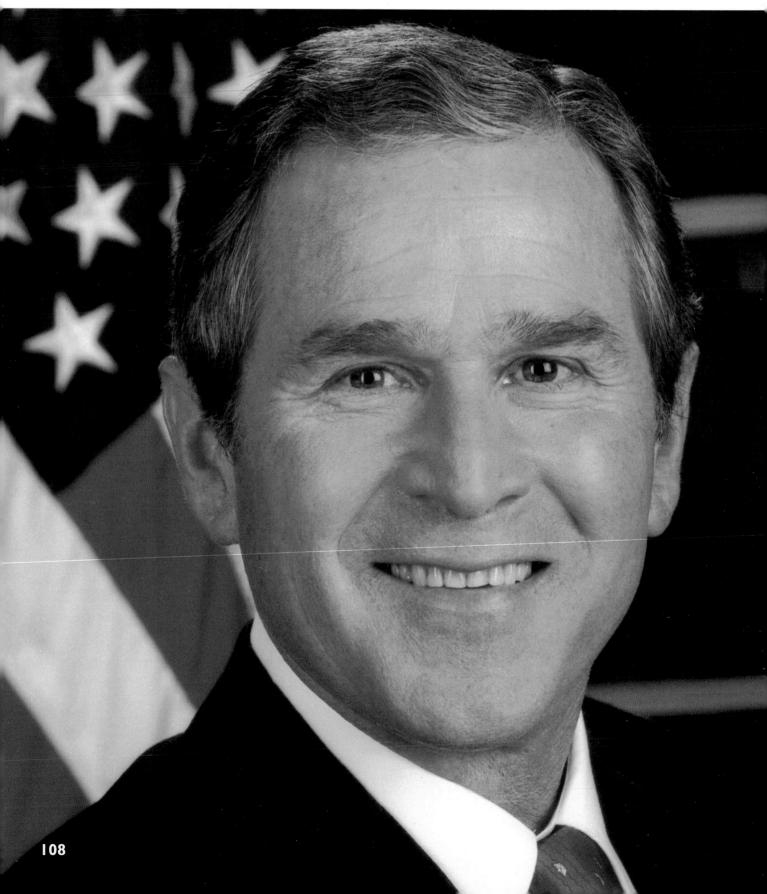

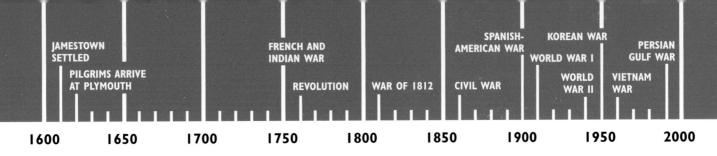

| JAMESTOWN SETTLED | | | FRENCH AND INDIAN WAR | | | | SPANISH-AMERICAN WAR | KOREAN WAR | PERSIAN GULF WAR |
| PILGRIMS ARRIVE AT PLYMOUTH | | | REVOLUTION | WAR OF 1812 | CIVIL WAR | | WORLD WAR I | WORLD WAR II | VIETNAM WAR |

1600   1650   1700   1750   1800   1850   1900   1950   2000

- **Born:** July 6, 1946, in New Haven, Connecticut
- **Education:** Graduated from Yale University in 1968 and Harvard Business School in 1975
- **Occupation:** Energy company executive, baseball club executive, governor
- **Political Party:** Republican
- **Vice-President:** Richard Cheney
- **Married:** 1977, to Laura Welch
- **Children:** Jenna and Barbara

Texas Governor George Walker Bush defeated Vice President Al Gore in the presidential race of 2000—one of the closest races in United States history. After being nominated by the Republican Party, Bush promised help for schools, tax cuts, and a revamped social security plan. His election allowed the Republican Party to reclaim the White House after eight years of Democratic rule.

Bush had chosen former defense secretary Richard Cheney as his running mate. Cheney brought extensive foreign policy and defense expertise to the ticket.

Although Gore offered a strong challenge in the presidential race, Bush campaigned as the candidate who would bring change. Bush narrowly won the election by four electoral votes. He did, however, lose the popular vote, which caused much controversy.

Because the results were so close, a recount was necessary in Florida, where the decisive electoral votes would be cast. It took more than two weeks for the recount to be conducted, and Bush was confirmed as the winner. Gore challenged the results, and the case was argued in the United States Supreme Court. The court voted 5-4 in favor of Bush.

THE FIRST LADY

Laura Welch Bush was a former librarian. In her role as First Lady, she worked to share her love of reading with Americans, especially young children. She earned a bachelor's degree in education from Southern Methodist University and a master's degree in library science from the University of Texas at Austin. She helped organize the Texas Book Festival in 1996, which became an annual fundraiser for Texas public libraries.

THE VICE-PRESIDENT

Richard B. Cheney was a businessman who served three presidents before becoming vice-president. He earned his bachelor's and master's degrees from the University of Wyoming. In 1969, he joined the Nixon Administration. In 1974, after Nixon's resignation, he served on the transition team of the Ford administration. Cheney was secretary of state during George H. W. Bush's presidency, and was awarded the Presidential Medal of Freedom on July 3, 1991.

IN BUSH'S DAY

2001: A damaged U.S. spy plane made an emergency landing at the Lingshui naval air base in China after colliding with a Chinese fighter jet. The Chinese pilot was killed and the 24-member American EP-3 crew was held for 11 days.

2001: A severe electrical power shortage caused blackouts and increased energy costs in California.

CHRONOLOGY

President:	Served:	Age at Inauguration:
1. George Washington	1789–1797	57
2. John Adams	1797–1801	61
3. Thomas Jefferson	1801–1809	57
4. James Madison	1809–1817	57
5. James Monroe	1817–1825	58
6. John Quincy Adams	1825–1829	57
7. Andrew Jackson	1829–1837	61
8. Martin Van Buren	1837–1841	54
9. William Henry Harrison	1841*	68
10. John Tyler	1841–1845	51
11. James Polk	1845–1849	49
12. Zachary Taylor	1849–1850*	64
13. Millard Fillmore	1850–1853	50
14. Franklin Pierce	1853–1857	48
15. James Buchanan	1857–1861	65
16. Abraham Lincoln	1861–1865*	52
17. Andrew Johnson	1865–1869	56
18. Ulysses S. Grant	1869–1877	46
19. Rutherford B. Hayes	1877–1881	54
20. James Garfield	1881*	49
21. Chester A. Arthur	1881–1885	50
22. Grover Cleveland	1885–1889	47
23. Benjamin Harrison	1889–1893	55
24. Grover Cleveland	1893–1897	55
25. William McKinley	1897–1901*	54
26. Theodore Roosevelt	1901–1909	42
27. William Howard Taft	1909–1913	51
28. Woodrow Wilson	1913–1921	56
29. Warren G. Harding	1921–1923*	55
30. Calvin Coolidge	1923–1929	51
31. Herbert Hoover	1929–1933	54
32. Franklin D. Roosevelt	1933–1945*	51
33. Harry S. Truman	1945–1953	60
34. Dwight D. Eisenhower	1953–1961	62
35. John F. Kennedy	1961–1963*	43
36. Lyndon B. Johnson	1963–1969	55
37. Richard M. Nixon	1969–1974**	56
38. Gerald Ford	1974–1977	61
39. Jimmy Carter	1977–1981	52
40. Ronald Reagan	1981–1989	69
41. George Bush	1989–1993	64
42. Bill Clinton	1993–2001	46
43. George W. Bush	2001–	55

* Died in office ** Resigned

FURTHER READING

Anderson, Marilyn D. *The Vice Presidency* (Your Government: How It Works). New York: Chelsea House Pub., 2001.

Bausum, Ann. *Our Country's Presidents.* Washington, D.C.: National Geographic Society, 2001.

Heath, David. *Elections in the United States* (American Civics). Mankato, MN: Bridgestone Books, 1999.

Kramer, Sydelle A. *The Look-It-Up-Book of First Ladies.* New York: Random House, 2001.

McNamara, Kevin J. *The Presidency* (Your Government: How It Works). New York: Chelsea House Pub., 2000.

Pastan, Amy. *Eyewitness: First Ladies.* New York: DK Publishing, 2001.

Sanders, Mark C. *The White House* (American Government Today). Chatham, NJ: Raintree/Steck Vaughn, 2001.

Sullivan, George. *Mr. President: A Book of U.S. Presidents* (Scholastic Biography). New York: Scholastic Trade, 2001.

Wellman, Sam. *The Cabinet* (Your Government: How It Works). New York: Chelsea House Pub., 2001.

INDEX